ENGLAND'S WITCHCRAFT TRIALS

For Jolyon and Oliver

ENGLAND'S WITCHCRAFT TRIALS

Willow Winsham

PEN & SWORD
HISTORY

First published in Great Britain in 2018 by
PEN AND SWORD HISTORY
an imprint of
Pen and Sword Books Ltd
47 Church Street
Barnsley
South Yorkshire S70 2AS

Copyright © Willow Winsham, 2018

ISBN 978 1 47387 094 9

The right of Willow Winsham to be identified
as the author of this work has been asserted by her in accordance
with the Copyright, Designs and Patents Act 1988.

A CIP record for this book is available from the British Library
All rights reserved. No part of this book may be reproduced or
transmitted in any form or by any means, electronic or
mechanical including photocopying, recording or
by any information storage and retrieval system, without
permission from the Publisher in writing.

Printed and bound in the UK
by T J International, Padstow, Cornwall, PL28 8RW

Typeset in Times New Roman 11/13.5 by
Aura Technology and Software Services, India

Pen & Sword Books Ltd incorporates the imprints of Pen & Sword
Archaeology, Atlas, Aviation, Battleground, Discovery,
Family History, History, Maritime, Military, Naval, Politics, Railways,
Select, Social History, Transport, True Crime, Claymore Press,
Frontline Books, Leo Cooper, Praetorian Press, Remember When,
Seaforth Publishing and Wharncliffe.

For a complete list of Pen and Sword titles please contact
Pen and Sword Books Limited
47 Church Street, Barnsley, South Yorkshire, S70 2AS, England
E-mail: enquiries@pen-and-sword.co.uk
Website: www.pen-and-sword.co.uk

Contents

Acknowledgements vi

List of Illustrations viii

Introduction xi

Chapter 1   Kill or Cure: St Osyth – 1582 1

Chapter 2   Possession and Posturing: The Witches
             of Warboys 1589–1593 24

Chapter 3   Families at War: The Pendle Witches – 1612 50

Chapter 4   The Witch-Finders: Bury St Edmunds – 1645 75

Chapter 5   Final Victims: The Bideford Witches – 1682 97

Afterword 117

Select Bibliography 118

Notes 121

Acknowledgements

As with the first, there were times when it seemed unlikely this book was ever going to happen at all, largely due to the fact that it was written during the pregnancy and early months of life of our third and very much non-sleeping child!

Just as with children, thankfully I did not have to go it alone, and a book isn't brought into being and nurtured in isolation. There are, as always, many people whom I need to thank for their support and input in making this the best book it can be and keeping me sane in the process.

Firstly, a huge and heartfelt thanks to my long-suffering husband, not least for helping create the time and space to carry out the work this book has needed. Thanks and love also to our children, Elizabeth, Alfred, and now Jolyon, for making our family all that it is and bringing so much meaning and happiness to my world. One day I hope you'll read these books and be proud of your history-obsessed mother.

I also need to thank:

Debbie Corlett, both for her many years of friendship and for the tireless and painstaking proofreading and suggestions which have helped make this book the best that it can be. Long may we continue to share interests and conversations regarding the correct or otherwise use of grammar.

An Victoir, simply for being herself and being there; I would not be able to believe in myself the way I do today without her having first shown me the way.

Two special thankyous go out to Amanda Capern, for planting the seeds of interest in 'women's' history many, many years ago. I might have eschewed witches in favour of eighteenth-century female reformers at the time, but

ACKNOWLEDGEMENTS

without the thorough grounding in the value of research, along with the encouragement and fanning of the flames of passion for 'getting it right', my books would not have been possible. Heartfelt thanks also to Dave Berger for many hours of support and at many times just listening; without him this and my previous book would literally not have come into being, as he gifted me the desk at which both have been written.

Further thanks go out to John Worland for his kind help and patience in answering my questions regarding the case of Ursula Kempe and for sharing his superb research. Malcolm Gaskill for likewise aiding in my digging on the Matthew Hopkins chapter and general help and encouragement. I am also in debt to Philip Almond for his permission to use his personal images and for discussion on details of the Warboys case.

This list wouldn't be complete without a massive shout-out to the #FolkloreThursday crowd. So many wonderfully kind, enthusiastic and fascinating individuals come together each week to share a passion for all things folklore, and it has truly been a privilege to get to know so many of them over the last two years. Thank you. And an extra special mention to Dee Dee Chainey, co-founder, friend, and sharer of many, many moments of hilarity, fun and misbehaving technology. I raise a badger in her honour.

Last but not least, I also extend thanks to the several archives and records offices that have aided in my research for this book, amongst them, Essex Record Office, Huntingdonshire Archives, Norfolk Record Office, Gary Knaggs of North Devon Record Office, John Monks of Exeter Civic Society, and various other individuals and organisations accessed throughout the course of my research. It has been a true pleasure, and I heartily hope I have done the original source material the justice it deserves.

Willow Winsham, August 2017.

List of Illustrations

Title page of *A True and Just Record*. (© Wellcome Library, London.)

1921 image of the St Osyth skeleton – 'Ursula'.

Examination of 'Ursula'. (© John Worland.)

Detail of nail fragment in 'Ursula' skeleton. (© John Worland.)

The Manor House at Warboys. (© Philip Almond.)

The Manor House at Warboys, side view. (© Philip Almond.)

Church of St Mary Magdelene, Warboys. (© Philip Almond.)

Interior of Huntingdon gaol. (© Philip Almond.)

Outside Hutingdon gaol. (© Philip Almond.)

Location of the Huntingdon gallows today. (© Philip Almond.)

Read Hall. (© Jennie Lee Cobban)

Lancaster Castle. (© Jennie Lee Cobban.)

Trough of Bowland. (© Jennie Lee Cobban.)

Ruins of a barn at Bull Hole Farm. (© Jennie Lee Cobban.)

Witches gathering for a meal with Devils. (© Wellcome Library, London.)

Rumoured Grave of Alice Nutter. (© Jennie Lee Cobban.)

LIST OF ILLUSTRATIONS

Matthew Hopkins. (© Wellcome Library, London.)

Eighteenth-century image of Matthew Hopkins. (© Wellcome Library, London.)

Matthew Hopkins with several familiars. (© Wellcome Library, London.)

Witch Swimming. (© Wellcome Library, London.)

Title Page of *An Historical Essay Concerning Witchcraft.* (© Wellcome Library, London.)

Burial Record for Matthew Hopkins D/P 343/1/1 (With permission of Essex Record Office.)

John Andrew's Trust Account Book entries for 1679 NDRO B1003/1/1 (With kind permission of North Devon Record Office and John Andrew Trust.)

John Andrew's Trust Account Book entries for 1680 and 1681 NDRO B1003/1/1 (With kind permission of North Devon Record Office and John Andrew Trust.)

Bideford Quarter Sessions Records, 1682 NDRO 1064Q-SQ-1 (With kind permission of North Devon Record Office.)

Close up of Bideford Quarter Sessions Records, 1682 (With kind permission of North Devon Record Office.)

Close up of Bideford Quarter Sessions Records, 1682 (With kind permission of North Devon Record Office.)

Witch Cottage, Bideford. (With kind permission of Bideford Library.)

Plaque Commemorating the Bideford Witches. 'Exeter Civic Society (www.exetercivicsociety.org.uk)'

Bideford Mural depicting Bideford Witches. 'Exeter Civic Society (www.exetercivicsociety.org.uk)'

Introduction

When I revealed to people that I was working on a second book, the first question was always 'What's *this* one on?' There was often surprise when I gave the answer 'More witches'. There have been many, many thousands of words already written about England's witch trials. There is always a danger therefore when trying to add something new to a well-worn subject, and the first consideration when setting out on such a project is whether anything can indeed be added to the historical conversation.

The answer is, I believe, a firm yes. It is an inexhaustible topic with limitless scope and interest, and there is a reason that the stories of those accused of witchcraft have kept the attention of readers for centuries.

This book looks at several of England's larger witchcraft trials, delving into the worlds of Ursula Kempe, The Witches of Warboys, The Pendle Witches, Matthew Hopkins, and the purported last witches executed in England, the three known to history as the Bideford Witches. These names are well known, their cases some of the most famous of the witch trials period. There is always something new to learn, some previously undiscovered nuance or fact, and although the ground is well trodden, there will at times be new paths taken and explored which bring a full and deep picture of the individuals involved and the cases as a whole.

Between the period of 1563 and 1736, England saw the rise and fall of belief in, and persecution of, those suspected of witchcraft. Less than 500 executions took place for the crime during that period, and yet they are a large part of England's history, and the belief in witches remains deeply entrenched even today, though with more positive connotations. The fear of witches led to deeds and actions that today seem inexplicable, but the fear was very, very real. Not only did witchcraft provide an explanation for the unexplainable, it ran deeper than that; often the facts of the past were rewritten or re-remembered and interpreted to fit a new situation, when social, political or religious tensions rose to boiling point and bubbled over. Perhaps in no other area of history are the very real fears, beliefs and values of ordinary people so clearly highlighted, the trial accounts and testimonies providing a fascinating and insightful reflection of society as a whole.

We will never know just how many individuals were accused of witchcraft or just how many were persecuted for the crime over the centuries. Here you will read of some of their stories, and in understanding their times and beliefs, learn just a little of what it might have been like to be persecuted for a witch.

Chapter 1

Kill or Cure: St Osyth – 1582

This I speak... upon a late view of trial,
taken against certain Witches in the county of Essex;
the orderly process in whose examinations,
together with other accidents,
I diligently observing and considering their
treacheries to be notable.

A True and Just Record, 1582

In the history of the English witch trials, Essex won for itself a certain prestige from the outset: the first execution for witchcraft in the country took place in Chelmsford in 1566, only three years after the new Witchcraft Act was passed.[1] It would prove to be a bad omen indeed, as the county bore the brunt of more than its fair share of witchcraft-related trials and bloodshed in the decades to follow, with many accused men and women ending their lives at the gallows.

In 1582 the village of St Osyth was to experience first-hand a wash of witchcraft accusations that would develop into one of the county's most infamous and well-recorded witch trials. As was so often the case, it started with a simple feud between two women: Grace Thurlow and Ursula Kempe, both long-term residents of St Osyth. Trouble had been brewing for some time, but finally came to a head when, on 19 February 1582, Grace spoke out against her one-time friend to Brian Darcy, a justice of the peace for Essex. Whether Grace had any inkling of where matters would end cannot be known, but that day she set in motion a chain of events that was to have disastrous consequences for the community in which the two women lived and worked.

Grace carefully related how, when her son Davy had been unwell the previous year, Ursula visited the Thurlow household to see how the boy was faring. The visit had passed amicably enough, with Ursula taking it upon herself to carry out a perhaps well-known folk-ritual in an attempt to help the sick child. Taking Davy's hand she had remarked, 'A good child how thou art loden,' before getting to her feet and leaving the house, only to return again a moment later to repeat her words to the child.[2] Grace had looked on as Ursula carried out this ritual three times in total, and it was clear that the worried mother had found comfort in the perceived meaning behind her friend's actions, asking Ursula to return to see them again that night. Ursula assented, assuring Grace that her son would now be on the mend, and her words proved true: the sick child passed the night in greater comfort than he had done since falling ill, much to the satisfaction of all concerned.

Grace was pregnant at the time and, due to the apparent good state of their friendship and her known experience in helping women in childbirth, Ursula had apparently – and erroneously – assumed that she would be asked to attend Grace when her time came. She was to be rudely disabused of this notion three months later as it transpired that Grace had arranged for another woman to assist her. Greatly angered, the snubbed Ursula had let Grace know her feelings on the matter in no uncertain terms, making it clear that she would not tolerate such a slight. This was the first sign that things were not as friendly between the two women as might have been assumed: as Grace remarked pointedly on a fit of lameness that had troubled her, issuing a barely veiled threat that, if she continued to suffer, she would go before a magistrate and name Ursula as the cause. Ursula, after all, had a 'naughty' name, and it might just be that Grace's lameness came from a not-so-natural cause.

Despite the potential seriousness of such an implication, Ursula had not seemed much bothered by Grace's threats, or the connection of her name with witchcraft. By her own admission in fact, she was capable of un-witching those who had been bewitched, but was not able to carry out bewitching herself. Ursula had then offered to show Grace how to un-witch herself and cure her own lameness: all Grace had to do was send away the unwanted birth attendant and she, Ursula, would help her.

Grace did not reveal to Darcy whether she had taken Ursula up on her offer, but the child, a girl, was delivered without incident. The two women clashed again shortly after the birth, this time over who would nurse the child. Perhaps on account of their recent disagreement, Grace did not hand over the task to Ursula, choosing instead to nurse her own child, even as she continued with her work as a maid. All seemed well – until tragedy struck: the baby, barely 3 months old, fell from her cradle and died of a broken neck. Far from expressing sympathy at this awful turn of events, Ursula had made it clear that the tragedy could have been avoided if only Grace had given her the child to nurse as she had asked.

Unsurprisingly, the two women remained at odds with each other, and the grieving mother found herself suffering again with the lameness that had previously bothered her. During this time, unbidden and unannounced, Ursula had come to the Thurlow house and told Grace she would cure her if her old friend would give her 12 pence.[3] Suffering greatly, Grace agreed, and for five weeks after Ursula's visit she felt great relief, from her physical suffering at least. When Ursula came to collect payment, Grace admitted that she had no money, and due to her poverty could not pay her. Ursula offered to take cheese in payment, but Grace had none of that either. This proved to be the last straw where their precarious friendship was concerned; after a heated exchange an angry Ursula left in high dudgeon.

Upon her departure, Grace fell lame once more, and continued to suffer from that day on. Matters were even worse than before, for the moment she began to show even a sign of improvement, the condition of Davy, her surviving child, grew worse; if *he* felt better, then Grace herself grew so lame she could not get out of bed.

All of this Grace Thurlow told the justice on that day in mid-February. The implication was clear: Ursula Kempe and her witchcraft were to blame for her suffering and the ills that had befallen herself and her children.

Grace was not the only one to speak out against Ursula. That same day, Agnes Letherdale did likewise, unburdening herself before the keenly listening justice. Agnes told Brian Darcy that Ursula had sent her son to ask her, Agnes, for some scouring sand.[4] In exchange, Ursula offered 'the dyeing of a pair of womens hose', but Agnes, 'knowing her to be a naughty beast sent her none'.[5] Agnes was happy to give the sand to others, and when her daughter was making a delivery elsewhere, Ursula happened to see the transaction take place. Again angered by such a slight, Ursula apparently muttered something inaudible – what her words were goes unrecorded, but shortly afterwards one of Agnes's children was struck with a strange and terrible illness, 'with a great swelling in the bottom of the belly, and other privy parts'.[6]

Agnes told Darcy that just over a week before her interview with him, she had approached Ursula, informing her that she had been to see a cunning man or woman to discover who or what was behind her child's suffering.[7] The answer was unequivocal: Ursula Kempe had bewitched the child. As with Grace Thurlow's account, Agnes related how Ursula had been unimpressed with this revelation, stating that not only had she done no such thing, but that she didn't believe Agnes had been to visit anyone in the first place. Agnes continued to believe in Ursula's culpability, and the child itself had provided further evidence to support what the cunning person had told her: on the way to visit Mother Ratcliffe, a woman known for her abilities to help those who were bewitched, the child had pointed towards the windows of Ursula's house, crying 'wo wo', plaintively as if making its own accusation.[8] This was no coincidence; the ill child had repeated the same gesture on the way home again. Despite being certain who was to blame, this knowledge had not done her child any good as its suffering had grown worse than ever, and even Mother Ratcliffe had not been confident that there was much to be done: the child continued to be in a bad state indeed at the very time Agnes was speaking with the justice.[9]

The day after Grace Thurlow and Agnes Letherdale spoke to Brian Darcy, Ursula herself was brought in to be questioned. In the account of what transpired the reader is left to imagine how Ursula felt at being summoned, and one wonders whether she was at first as assured and unworried as she was reported to have been when the two women accused her of witchcraft to her face. First Ursula told Darcy that about ten or eleven years earlier she had herself suffered a bout of lameness. In order to find a cure, she had visited the wife of a man named Cock, in Weeley, a village five miles north of St Osyth.[10] The woman had told Ursula that she had been bewitched, and when Ursula in turn begged to be taught how to cure herself, Cock's wife had obliged. She had told Ursula that the best method was to mix some hog's dung and charvell together, then, holding this in her left hand and a knife in the other, she should prick the medicine three times before throwing it into the fire.[11] After doing so, she should then make three pricks under a table, before sticking the knife there. Finally, she was to take three sage leaves and the same amount of 'herb John' and put them in ale.[12] This was to be drunk first thing in the morning and last thing at night, and if the directions were followed properly, Ursula would find herself well.

The cure was duly carried out and Ursula had found her condition much improved. Not wanting to keep this new-found knowledge to herself, Ursula decided to use it to help others. The wives of Page and Gray, women also suffering from lameness, had sent for her and, after declaring them bewitched, Ursula had given them both the same cure that she had taken. Much to the satisfaction of all, both women had soon become well again.

It seems that Ursula had been talking quite freely up to this point, but Darcy remained unimpressed. She had not, after all, touched upon the matter that had brought her before him: the alleged bewitchment of the children of Grace Thurlow and Agnes Letherdale. The Justice was not a man without resources and at this point in the interview, Brian Darcy made Ursula a promise. If she would speak the whole truth and make a proper confession, he told her, she need have nothing to fear – she would be treated leniently.

If the account is to be believed, now came the first hint that Ursula was not as calm as she had first appeared. At Darcy's words she burst into tears, the floodgates opening as Ursula fell to her knees before the justice.

In the confession that followed she told Darcy that she had four familiar spirits, two male and two female. The female spirits caused lameness and other bodily harm to those of her choosing, and were also used to harm cattle. The males were altogether more dangerous, and brought death to those Ursula decided to punish. Pressed further, she gave descriptions of her devilish helpers: one of the males was like a grey cat and called Titty, whilst the other male was a black cat called Jack. The females were Piggin, a black toad, and Tiffin, a white lamb. When asked which spirits she had sent to Grace Thurlow and to Agnes Letherdale's child, Ursula said that Titty had gone to Grace, and Piggin to the child. She also confessed to having sent Tiffin to knock over the Thurlow cradle, leading to the accident that caused the death of Grace's baby.

Still greatly distressed and apparently without further prompting, Ursula went on to confess that she had caused the death of her own sister-in-law, her brother's wife, by sending Jack to torment her to death in retaliation for calling her a witch and a whore.

Darcy could be well-pleased with himself for extracting such a confession, albeit through less than honest means, as it would later transpire. There was more to come, which may or may not have been foreseen by the Justice. As Grace Thurlow and Agnes Letherdale were present in the house, the two women were brought into the room to confront their supposed tormentor. Upon seeing them, Ursula again fell to her knees and begged their forgiveness, but that was not all; her next words incriminated another local woman, Alice Newman. According to Ursula, at her bidding Alice had sent spirits to plague both Agnes's child and Grace Thurlow, and was thus as caught up in the matter as Ursula herself.

Despite her confession, Ursula appears to have undergone a change of heart overnight, as the next day she spoke with Darcy again, under the pretext of having forgotten to mention something in her previous interview. This time her story was subtly different; about a quarter of a year earlier Alice Newman had come to Ursula's house, where the two women had quarrelled. The exact cause was not made clear, but Ursula recounted how, during the altercation, Alice had called her a witch and threatened to report her to Darcy himself. It was yet another threat that Ursula did not take seriously, especially as, after their harsh exchange of words, the two became friends once more and were on good terms by the time Alice left later that day. Alice did not return home alone; according to Ursula, she had left her house carrying none other than Ursula's spirits in a pot.

The two women had continued as friends and at Christmas time that year, Ursula had told Alice of her falling out with Grace Thurlow. She had also, she admitted, asked Alice to send the spirit Titty to plague Grace and cause her suffering. Alice had willingly done so, and when the spirit returned it told Ursula that it had done as requested. Ursula had therefore rewarded Titty by allowing it to suck blood from her before the spirit returned to Alice.

During this second interview, Ursula went on to tell Darcy of further disputes with her neighbours: John Stratton had called her names, and his wife had also refused to give spices to Ursula's son when he had requested them. In response to these slights, Ursula had again approached Alice, asking her to send the spirit Jack to John Stratton's wife. This spirit did as it was bidden, and was rewarded twice: by some blood from Ursula's thigh and also by Alice Newman.

In this second confession Ursula had carefully shifted culpability from herself to Alice, no doubt hoping to make good on Darcy's promise of leniency by offering another in her place. Accordingly, Alice Newman herself was examined that same day, giving her version of events in response to Ursula's revelations. According to Alice, she had indeed been at Ursula's house on the day in question, and the two women had fallen out as Ursula had related. She had also, she admitted, told Ursula that she knew her to be a witch, but stubbornly denied everything else that Ursula had said occurred between them, including knowing anything about the spirits she was supposed to have in her possession. Despite her protestations, Alice made a telling mistake: when threatened by Darcy with the removal of her spirits if she did not cooperate, she replied that such a thing could not happen, as she would keep them with her. The hastily added qualification that this would only be the case if she had any spirits in the first place was not quite enough to undo the incriminating assertion, a triumph that Darcy no doubt savoured. The witch hunt had begun.

It was now a case of finding further evidence against the accused women, a task that Darcy rose to with enthusiasm. Alice's neighbour, William Hook, spoke out freely against her. He told Darcy how he had heard Alice's husband William Newman blame Alice for his current misery, though what form that misery took was not elaborated upon. William Hook had also overheard a curious exchange take place between the couple at meal times on several occasions. Whenever meat was served, William Newman could be heard to demand, 'doest thou not see?', implying, Hook told the Justice, that something untoward was in the room.[13] Alice always responded in the same way, telling her husband that if he saw anything, he should just give 'it' some meat and it would go away again. This did not, according to Hook, seem to have solved the problem as William Newman had later been heard to tell his wife to beat the thing – whatever it was – away.[14]

Ursula herself was most obliging and made yet another confession, during which she incriminated several further women: Elizabeth Bennett, Alice Hunt and Agnes Glascock. Elizabeth Bennett, said Ursula, kept a spirit in the shape of a ferret in a pot; she knew this because about three months earlier she had visited her to ask for some milk and had spotted the creature as she peered through the window to see whether Elizabeth was at home. Elizabeth had two spirits in total and their names were Suckin and Lierd; when asked how she knew this, Ursula replied that the spirit Tiffin, of whom she once again claimed ownership, had told her. Elizabeth was responsible for plaguing the wife of a man named Byatt to death, and also making three of his cattle very ill – two had died, the third being saved only by the lighting of a fire around the creature who then tried to flee from the heat. Elizabeth's actions extended further than malice towards livestock: she had sent a spirit to torment the child of a man named Fortune, and was also responsible for the deaths of a man named Willingale, and the wife of William Willes, who had suffered for many years before finally succumbing.

Elizabeth Bennett was not the only one to have a ferret-shaped spirit. Ursula paid a visit to Alice Hunt back in January and on finding no one at home, had peered into a window and spotted a spirit much the same as she had described at the Bennett house, likewise kept under a cloth in a pot. Tiffin again informed Ursula of what this spirit had been used for, revealing that six beasts belonging to a man named Hayward had been killed by it at Alice Hunt's behest. Alice had, according to Tiffin, rewarded the spirit with some blood, although the location this was taken from was unknown to Ursula as she had not been told.

As for Agnes Glascock, Ursula had been informed by a local shoemaker named Michell that he believed Agnes had bewitched his child and was responsible for its death. When Ursula asked Tiffin if this was true, the spirit confirmed that it was, and that Agnes had sent one of the spirits in her possession to torment the child to death. Agnes was also responsible for the death of a child that had been in the care of Page and his wife.

Ursula concluded with further incriminating words against Alice Newman. She related how Alice had gone to visit Johnson, the man responsible for collecting and distributing money to the poor, to ask for 12 pence to help her sick husband. Johnson had not been able to grant the request and Alice had responded angrily, an argument erupting between the pair. In revenge, Alice had sent one of her spirits to both Johnson and his wife, with the intent of tormenting them to death.

The first to be accused, Ursula had in turn become an informer, incriminating several local women in an attempt to provide Darcy with what he wanted and in so doing, she believed she would save herself. As most of the information she imparted came through her spirit Tiffin, Ursula was questioned regarding the honesty of this spirit; it had, she avowed, always spoken the truth to the best of her knowledge, and she had not related anything she had reason to suspect was untrue. As a direct result of Ursula's spirit-inspired revelations, several of those she named were apprehended and brought in for questioning.

Agnes Glascock was greatly unimpressed by her treatment and denied the accusations made against her. This did not save her from being searched, and spots were discovered on the left side of her thigh and also on her left shoulder.[15] Faced with Agnes's persistent denial and perhaps hoping to force her into confessing, Darcy orchestrated matters so that Agnes Glascock and Ursula were brought into the same room, where Ursula made her accusations against the other woman to her face. Far from obliging, Agnes exploded; using 'outrageous' words in her fury, she called Ursula a whore, threatening to scratch her like the witch she was.[16] The irate Agnes went on to claim that far from being guilty herself, she was in fact a victim, as Ursula had made it so that she, Agnes, could not cry, certain proof that the other woman had bewitched her.[17]

Alice Hunt likewise denied Ursula's accusations, insisting that she had not fallen out with Hayward and that she had neither plagued cattle nor kept a spirit in a pot. A pot was brought before her and she was asked again whether she fed her spirits from it; Alice insisted that she did not and that the pot was not hers. Such denials did her little good, and a warrant was drawn up to have her arrested. Desperate, Alice took her cue from Ursula and asked to speak with Darcy alone; doing so she tearfully confessed to him on her knees, admitting that she did in fact have two spirits who had visited her as little as six days ago. They were named Jack and Robin, and took the form of small colts; one was black and the other was white. Not only that, but they had told her that Ursula would betray her, and now that prediction had come true. Alice was not the only member of the Hunt family to be dabbling with witchcraft either; her sister, Margery Sammon, had two spirits of her own. Alice finished her account by telling Darcy of these two creatures, both in the form of toads and named Tom and Robin. It was no coincidence that the sisters had these spirits; they had received them from their mother, Mother Barnes, a witch herself, who had died less than a fortnight earlier. Margery Sammon was duly questioned and despite initially refusing to say anything, after persuasion from her sister she admitted to possessing the two spirits.

In such a heightened atmosphere, the sense of suspicion and mounting fear within the St Osyth community must have been too much for some to bear. It is not surprising, therefore, to find in some cases the accused following Ursula's example and becoming in turn the accuser in face of Darcy's understandably persuasive promises of leniency to those who cooperated; first Ursula herself and then sisters Alice Hunt and Margery Sammon turned on other local women in the hope of deflecting attention from themselves. In her examination before Darcy, Margery implicated the widowed Joan Pechey; her mother had told her that if she did not wish to keep the spirits she should send them to Joan. Afraid of being apprehended after learning of Ursula's arrest, she had duly sent them away to be received by the other woman and that had been the last she had seen of them. Alice Hunt also spoke against Joan; living next door, she had heard Joan talking when there was no one else in the house with her – therefore she must have been talking to her imps. Her mother had also told her that Joan was skilled at witchcraft, and Alice believed her to be even more skilled than her mother had been. Indeed Joan was said to have the power to know everything that took place in every house in St Osyth, something she used to her advantage.

It was hardly surprising that Joan Pechey was taken in for questioning, though if Darcy was hoping for another confession to add to his collection he was to be sadly disappointed: Joan utterly denied being a witch. Furthermore, she had no spirits, and certainly hadn't given them to, or got them from, Mother Barnes who, she was sure, had no reputation for being a witch. Joan also denied the rumour that she knew what anyone within the village was doing, she could do nothing of the sort.

When asked what she thought of the matter of the sudden death of Johnson the poor collector, Joan agreed that his death had been sudden and unexpected. She had also heard that a man named Lurkin had heard Johnson himself say that Alice Newman had bewitched him, supporting what Ursula had said in her most recent confession.[18]

Over the remainder of February and well into the following month, Darcy gathered more information from the inhabitants of St Osyth, as each new round of questioning brought forth fresh names and further evidence against those who had already been incriminated. Amongst them, Alice Hunt's daughter and Ursula's son both spoke out against their mothers, confirming what others had said about them and adding further delicious details. Henry and Cicely Sellis were amongst the newly accused, implicated in an arson attack on Ross's barn which was said to have been carried out by witchcraft. Cicely was also accused of causing the death of a child, tormenting the daughter of Thomas Death, and causing his swine to behave in a most peculiar fashion.

The web of accusations began to spill out of St Osyth to further afield, with Alice Manfield from nearby Thorpe implicated by a local constable for causing his cart to become stuck in the ground after a disagreement. Alice herself confessed to possessing spirits, called Robin, William, Jack and Puppet, which she sent out for a variety of nefarious purposes. With the number of suspected and accused witches growing by the day, no one, it seemed, was safe.

By early March, Ursula had been transferred to the gaol at Colchester Castle, and several others from the pool of the accused were soon to follow.[19] It is likely that with this development, she was now somewhat less sure of her protected status, despite Darcy's previous promise of leniency. Despite, or perhaps precisely because of this fact, Ursula continued to talk, naming names and incidents to anyone who would listen. One of her more outrageous claims was examined on 9 March, when it was put to Ursula that she had been telling several people who had visited her that Alice Newman had sent a spirit to the late Lord Darcy (who happened to have been a relation of Brian Darcy himself), which had been the cause of his death.

It is unclear just how many curious visitors came to Colchester to see the imprisoned witches, but Henry Durrant, a butcher from St Osyth, revealed that on 2 March he and several others had visited Ursula whilst in the town. Durrant had good reason to want to speak to this fount of information, and he quizzed Ursula closely on the death of his daughter, which he suspected had a sinister cause. Ursula obligingly told him that Alice Hunt and her mother, Mother Barnes, had bewitched the girl to death after Durrant had refused the two women pork when they asked for it, thus confirming the man's suspicions and fears.[20]

One of the last to give evidence was Lawrence Kempe, Ursula's own brother, who spoke out against her on 20 March. His wife, Ursula's sister-in-law, had been troubled in her back and in her 'privie parts' and had been very ill for the space of nine months before dying of her strange illness.[21] She had informed him on several occasions during that time that Ursula was the cause, and that the other woman had 'forspoke her'.[22] The animosity between Ursula and Mrs Kempe had been long standing; two years before her death the pair had a physical altercation on Eliots Heath, though the cause of it is unclear in the account. Despite this, Ursula was present at her sister-in-law's deathbed, although this fact was used ultimately as further proof against her. The fading woman had lingered for a day and a night before Ursula arrived uninvited: when she took her by the arm, Kempe related, his wife had gasped, before dying that very moment.

As the month drew to a close, those who had been arrested in the tide of accusation and counter-accusation passed their days in prison as they awaited trial. Ursula Kempe, Alice Newman, Alice Hunt and Elizabeth Bennett were all detained and, along with Cicely Sellis, Alice Mansfeld, Margaret Grevell, Agnes Glascock, Agnes Herd and several others, were tried at the Chelmsford Assizes on 29 March 1582, accused of various crimes.

Ursula and Alice Newman were indicted for murder by witchcraft, the official record declaring that, 'On 12 Feb 1582 at St Osyth they bewitched Elizabeth daughter of Richard Letherdale so that she died on 26 Feb,' and also that 'On 30 Nov 1581 at St Osyth they bewitched Edena wife of John Stratton so that she died on 14 Feb 1582.'[23] Furthermore, the pair were indicted for bewitching John and Grace Thurlow's daughter Joan on 3 October 1581 so that she died three days later. Alice Newman was remanded, but, despite the promised leniency for her cooperation, Ursula Kempe was found guilty and condemned to hang.[24]

Elizabeth Bennett was also found guilty of murder by witchcraft: she stood accused of bewitching William Byet and his wife Joan on 1 October 1581, finally causing their deaths four months later on 10 February 1582, and went to the gallows with Ursula.

Of the others who remained, Alice Hunt was found not guilty of murdering cattle belonging to William Hayward, or causing the death of Henry Durrant's daughter. Agnes Glascock was found guilty of several counts of murder by witchcraft, but was remanded and thus escaped the noose.

The elderly Joan Pechey was not tried, but was instead discharged by proclamation. This did not help her, and the old woman died in gaol before she could be released. Agnes Herd was found not guilty of the charges made against her, as was Margaret Grevell.

Cicely Sellis was not quite so lucky; she was cleared of the arson charge against her, but found guilty of bewitching the son of Thomas Death until he died: Cicely remained in prison on remand, only to die before she could be released, another victim of the terrible conditions of prisons of that time and the illness that was rife there.

The remanded Alice Newman was still in prison on 2 August 1582 along with Alice Hunt and Cicely Sellis. The last trace of Alice Newman is the prisoner list for 4 March 1588 at the Chelmsford Assizes; at the next Assizes on 15 June she is conspicuous only by her absence, and, as there is no record of her being discharged, it is probable that she too perished during her long imprisonment.

****

The main source for the tragic events at St Osyth is the wordily titled pamphlet *A true and just Record, of the Information, Examination and Confession of all the Witches, taken at S. Oses [sic] in the county of Essex: whereof some were executed, and other some entreated according to the determination of law.* As the title suggests, it is a remarkable piece of work indeed: the sheer length alone makes it stand out amongst other accounts of the period and, coming in at over a hundred pages long, it earns the distinction of being the longest witch trial pamphlet in existence at the time.[25] Made up of examinations and confessions taken from accusers and the accused pre-trial, the document provides a tantalisingly accurate record of the evidence that would have been presented in court when the case came before the Assizes, along with providing a stark portrait of how rumour and resentment could lead to the trial of fourteen women and the execution of two.

Essex was no stranger to accusations of witchcraft during the period of the witch trials; out of around 424 villages in the county in the sixteenth and seventeenth centuries, it is believed that over half saw accusations and prosecutions for witchcraft related crimes, coming second only to theft in terms of frequency.[26] The St Osyth trial was hugely influential where witchcraft belief was concerned, marking as it did the second major witch trial since witchcraft became a felony in England. St Osyth also had one of the highest casualty rates of the witch-hunt era in the Essex area and this exerted considerable influence in shaping the history of witchcraft persecution; Reginald Scott's seminal *Discoverie* was written in part as a result of the events that took place there, and more recently, Margaret Murray attempted to use the St Osyth case to prove her theory about covens being organised into groups of thirteen.[27]

There is no doubt that Ursula Kempe – alias Grey – takes centre stage in the drama that played out in St Osyth.[28] She was the first, and the most named, out of those who became caught up in the web of accusation and counter accusation, and also stands out as the individual to single-handedly accuse the most people in her turn. Although she spoke out against many of her neighbours to Darcy, this does not necessarily reflect a vindictive nature. Indeed, the Justice's promise of leniency rather than a desire to incriminate others may well have been behind her willingness to do so; if this is the case, her ploy failed disastrously, seeing Ursula go to the noose whilst many of those she had named went free.

By her own admission Ursula's relations with many of her neighbours in St Osyth were rocky to say the least, and by other accounts it is clear that she was considered to be volatile and quick to wrathfulness. Not only that, but several people in St Osyth 'knew' Ursula to be a witch; Grace Thurlow, Agnes Letherdale and Alice Newman all said as much and, despite Ursula herself being initially unconcerned when she was called a witch to her face, she eventually admitted to, and played into, the part assigned to her.

Interestingly, it is clear that Ursula held a dual role within the community and the imaginations of those who lived out their daily lives together.

Despite being eventually branded a witch, Ursula was also known for her ability to un-witch, thereby 'curing' the victims of bewitchment rather than causing such bewitchment herself. The turning of popular opinion against her highlights the precarious and often fatally ambiguous role held by those who professed to be able to cure others through magical means; the one who had previously been called upon to help could, during times of unrest and friction, be cast into the new role of enemy.

The mention in the account of Ursula assisting at births has often been erroneously interpreted to mean that she served as midwife in the St Osyth community, and is subsequently used as an explanation for the animosity against her, as midwives are generally perceived to have been one of the main groups that were persecuted during the witch-trial period. From the evidence available, it is clear that Ursula did indeed serve a role in attending local women during childbirth and also acted in the capacity of wet-nurse. This does not make her a midwife of either the licensed or non-licensed variety, and it is only in later accounts of the St Osyth trial that this conflation is made.[29] Far from being exploited as further proof of Ursula's motivation or ability to harm her victims, her role as birth attendant is almost ignored in the evidence given against her; it is the arguments with Grace Thurlow and others rather than an abuse of her supposed position that is given as the reason for her to have cause to do her supposed victims harm.

Regardless of Ursula's role within her community, it is also clear that far from being part of a largely persecuted group, 'midwives were generally immune from witchcraft prosecutions.'[30] In sharp contrast to the popular misconception, midwives were actually highly valued members of society, and were more often used as witnesses in court than finding themselves in the position of being accused. Furthermore, where witchcraft cases are concerned, there is a decidedly striking lack of references to midwives coming under suspicion at all: there is, in fact, only one documented case of a midwife being accused of witchcraft in England during the period of the witch trials. Mrs Pepper from Newcastle was accused of witchcraft at York Castle in 1665; although a midwife by profession, the accusations made against her were entirely unconnected to her role, and this therefore serves as further evidence that midwifery and witchcraft did not go hand-in-hand as has so often been suggested.[31]

The pamphlet account of events in St Osyth suggests that it was the falling out between Grace Thurlow and Ursula Kempe that spurred the initial accusations against Ursula and therefore set in motion the terrible chain of events that led her to the gallows. Indeed, Davy Thurlow falling ill around February 1581 marks the start of a steady build of suspicion, resentment and disagreements within the village. By that summer, Grace's newborn child was dead, Grace herself was experiencing lameness, and the two argued once more over Grace's inability to pay Ursula for the cure she had received. Throughout the autumn Ursula likewise fell out with Agnes Letherdale over the scouring sand and her child fell ill, Ursula fell out with Alice Newman (though the two were reconciled) and John Stratton called Ursula a whore. All of this paints a picture of a community experiencing a series of tensions, bubbling along throughout the year preceding the trial. This was a picture that could represent relationships within many a sixteenth-century village; what, then, pushed matters over the edge in this particular instance?

There has been some suggestion that Darcy himself may have been part of a wider attempt to root out witches in the area, potentially exploiting local gossip and that uttered amongst his own employees to achieve this aim. Grace Thurlow worked for Darcy, as did others from the village, and it is possible that he was not above using this to further his own agenda.[32] Grace's privileged and protected position as Darcy's employee might also explain why she herself was not accused as events unfolded.

There are also the intriguing details that emerge from the confessions and accusations made by Ursula and her neighbours regarding the death of Johnson, the local collector for the poor. Events and rumours surrounding his death may well have acted as a spark to fully ignite the flame of unrest in St Osyth, rather than letting the various neighbourly disagreements fizzle out. It was related by Ursula that around November or December 1581, Alice Newman had sent her spirits to plague Johnson and his wife to death. Although the exact date of their deaths is unknown, they must have taken place between this time and early February 1582; occurring in the midst of an already unsettled situation and with emotions running high, it could well have been the catalyst necessary for existing tensions to erupt.

The first mention of Johnson was in Ursula's second examination on 21 February, when she related how Alice Newman had visited Johnson to ask for 12 pence to help her sick husband, only to be refused, an act that prompted Alice to send her spirits to kill both Johnson and his wife. Johnson is again mentioned on 24 February, this time by Alice Hunt who revealed that Joan Pechey had been displeased with the quality of the beef and bread that she had been given by Johnson, saying that the latter was too hard for her teeth and that it should have been given to someone younger and better able to chew it. Elizabeth Bennett said that she herself had never sent spirits to Johnson (which implies that she had been accused of doing so, perhaps in a missing document) and neither, as far as she knew, had Alice Newman. However, she had been at Johnson's house once with some wool to spin as Johnson, also working as a cloth maker, often gave her work. It was during this time that Alice Newman had arrived to make her request for money, and therefore she had witnessed the altercation that followed. Joan Pechey only remarked that Johnson's death had been sudden and unexpected, and that she had never spoken against him, although she did repeat the rumour that Johnson was under the impression that Alice Newman had bewitched him. Ursula's son Thomas also agreed that Alice Newman had admitted to plaguing Johnson and his wife to death.

It seems, therefore, that there had been more than one person grumbling against Johnson, and perhaps, despite Joan Pechey's assertions, he was not an easy man to get along with. It is also highly likely that Johnson spoke the truth, and there simply was not food nor money enough to satisfy the growing number of poor in St Osyth and in the country as a whole.[33] The sudden death of a prominent figure within the community – whether liked or disliked – would have been felt by the whole village, and, with such a catalyst, accusations and gossip had the potential to grow and spread at alarming speed, something that Darcy may well have used to his advantage.

In this hotbed of rising recriminations, Agnes Letherdale confronted Ursula in early February 1582 with her accusations, Alice Newman allegedly sent her spirits to torment Agnes's child, and before the month was through, Grace and Agnes had officially complained against Ursula to the local justice.[34]

The nature of the accusations the women of St Osyth made against each other is instantly recognisable to anyone familiar with such accounts; fitting into a stock set of maleficium they can be broadly summed up as: causing illness and death to children, causing illness and death to those who had displeased them through denial of goods or services, the bewitchment of animals and the ruining of baking or brewing upon which the household depended. These reflected both popular witchcraft beliefs and also the anxieties and fears of the people of the time, a tantalising glimpse into the world of the sixteenth-century village community where explanations were demanded when illness and disease appeared to strike with neither rhyme nor reason. By the latter stage of the examinations it is evident that those involved were buying into the constructed narrative and potentially leading questions from Darcy himself, resulting in every coincidental mishap that had taken place in the previous few years being blamed on a witch. One good example of this is the case of John Sawyer, the Thorpe constable who swore Alice Manfield bewitched his cart after he declined to allow a thatcher working for him to thatch her oven. The fact of the disagreement coupled with the added coincidence that it happened to take place outside Alice's front door, was enough to convince him that the cause was witchcraft.

Another telling example involves Henry and Cicely Sellis. There had been several disagreements between the Sellis family and that of Richard Ross of Little Clacton, including the usual refusal of goods, in this case due to Cicely apparently being unwilling to pay the full price for the malt she had requested. Amidst the frictions of the St Osyth accusations, this, it seemed clear, gave Cicely the perfect motivation for getting her revenge, especially when the offences of speaking of a child shortly before it died and causing a maid of Richard Ross's to fall ill were added into the mix. Finally Cicely, her husband and her son Robert, were indicted for arson, through the burning down of a granary belonging to Ross on the night of 31 August 1581.[35] This case also illustrates the long-burning nature of disagreements; an incident with Henry Sellis and the mysterious death of Ross's horses occurred, according to Ross, six years previously, but were still brought up in relation to the current state of affairs, relevant now in the reinterpretation of events that was taking place.

The role of familiar spirits or imps is also integral to the St Osyth narrative, and again emphasises the community nature of the case. It is interesting to see that certain aspects, such as the keeping of a familiar in a pot on a bed of wool, that were present in the first witch trial of Agnes Waterhouse, appear again here in the St Osyth pamphlet, having entered into witchcraft-lore in the preceding decade-and-a-half. Despite the prevalence of imps in the narrative, these familiars are noticeably absent from the first two accounts taken, those of Grace Thurlow and Agnes Letherdale. Neither woman mentions imps of any sort in their initial accusations against Ursula, with both focusing instead on the arguments they had with her and the illnesses that followed. The first mention of spirits in fact was made by Ursula herself during her first examination by Darcy, the day after she was accused by Grace and Agnes. The question is obvious and a vital one: did Ursula supply the information entirely of her own volition (the fact that the account states that she spoke of them 'without any asking, of her own free will', immediately rouses suspicion) or was she in fact responding to leading questions or suggestions from Darcy that have gone unrecorded?[36]

The problem with such accounts is that they were invariably written and recorded by those who can hardly be said to have been impartial, and in very few cases is sympathy shown for the accused. Anything that might therefore be in their favour, or hint that the procedure followed was not entirely above board, would often, unhelpfully in an investigation into the truth, be altered or omitted altogether. In Ursula's case it is highly probable that she told the justice what he wanted to hear in response to, purposefully or subconsciously, leading questions from Darcy. The account plainly states that:

> The said Brian Darcy then promising to the said Ursula that if she would deal plainly and confess the truth, that she should have favour; and so by giving her fair speeches she confessed as followeth.[37]

What exactly did Darcy say to persuade Ursula to confess she had used spirits to harm her friends and neighbours? It is virtually impossible at this far remove to hazard more than speculation in that direction, or to know how much the 'evidence' given reflected Darcy's views of such creatures or those of the villagers. Once they entered the narrative the spirits were there to stay, with examination after examination of various witnesses repeating and embellishing what had been said before until no one could doubt their existence.

The imps or spirits in St Osyth came in a variety of forms. Ursula herself had two cats, a lamb and a toad, and it was these imps that she apparently shared with Alice Newman. Alice Hunt's step-daughter described her spirits as being 'two little things like horses', one black and the other white.[38] Ferrets also played a prominent part in the story, with several spirits being described as taking this form. The spirits required feeding, and were often rewarded for their services by small drops of blood from their owners. Although used primarily to cause torment and get revenge on those who had angered the women who sent them out, the spirits also passed on information at times, warning of impending discovery and condemnation. It is again interesting to note that such elements were present at the start of the period during which such cases were recorded, indicating that familiars had – unlike on the Continent – been fully embraced into the English witchcraft narrative.

The familiars also played another important role: that of allowing the accused to distance themselves from what they were confessing to have done. It was, after all, the spirit rather than the accused who had done the actual deed, albeit at her behest, and it was also the spirits that so helpfully kept rumours spreading, informing their mistresses of what was being said by, and about, others.[39]

Another question that one cannot help but ask is what, if anything, were people actually seeing and referring to in their descriptions of these spirits that were plaguing the good people of St Osyth? Given the frequency with which they were mentioned it is tempting to assume that creatures of some sort were indeed witnessed, although their origin must be carefully scrutinised. Were these simply normal household pets or pests that were being interpreted afresh in a sinister and deadly light? Did both accusers and accused really believe they were dealing with spirits in their midst? Or, was the leading nature of the questions put to them enough to have people claiming to have seen things they had not, in an attempt to fit with a discourse they recognised but did not fully understand?[40]

The use of child witnesses whose evidence was turned against the accused women is striking in the St Osyth case, with several examples of evidence being accepted from those who were legally under the age where their word could be accepted in court.[41] Thomas Rabbet, Ursula's 8-year-old 'base' son gave evidence against his mother, saying that, amongst other things, he had seen his mother feed her spirits with white bread and beer and also that they sucked her blood.[42] Thomas confirmed that his mother had four spirits, obligingly repeating their names and their colours as stated by other witnesses and Ursula. The boy was asked if Alice Newman had visited his mother, he confirmed that she had and that he had witnessed the two women falling out. They had made up their quarrel and Alice Newman had taken away the pot containing his mother's spirits. The bite was in the end of the boy's testimony: a few days later Alice Newman had come to see his mother, telling her that she had sent spirits to plague both Johnson and his wife.

Likewise, Alice Hunt's 8-year-old stepdaughter Phoebe spoke out against her, describing Alice's spirits and the fact that they were kept in a pot with wool, the wool also being black and white like the spirits. Phoebe had witnessed her stepmother feeding these creatures with milk from a wooden tray, and when the girl was taken by the constables to her house, she proceeded to identify the tray, and told how her mother had instructed her not to tell anyone about the matter.[43]

Nine-year-old Henry Sellis and his brother 6-year-old John both told how their mother Cicely had spirits which she fed, and also that she had told them not to mention the fact to anyone.[44] Agnes Dowsing was only 7 when she gave evidence against her mother, Agnes Herd, informing Darcy that she had six spirits in the form of blackbirds kept in one box, and another six that were in the shape of cows the size of rats.[45] Although not even able to speak, Agnes Letherdale's child pointing in the direction of Ursula's house and saying 'wo wo' was taken as evidence for her guilt, and it was this very incident, if her word is to be believed, that made Agnes go to Darcy in the first place to speak out against Ursula.[46]

The fate of these children, and their feelings about what their words eventually led to, can only be left open to conjecture. Like those who made accusations in the Salem Witch Trials, it is likely that the children had mixed responses to their part in the accusations and condemnations that took place; some would feel guilt and remorse, whilst others moved on unscathed.

As is common in accounts of those accused of witchcraft, sexual immorality, whether real or imagined, is an important part of the St Osyth narrative. Ursula and her reputation for being 'naughty' is no doubt connected to and enhanced by her having an illegitimate son. Joan Pechey was accused of incest with Phillip Barrenger, her own son; she had, it was said, made the 23-year-old man have intercourse with her. Joan herself denied this, saying that whilst she had her son lie in bed with her at times, it was not in any sexual way. Philip said otherwise, and 'confesseth and saith, that many times and of late he hath lain in naked bed with his own mother, being willed and commanded to doe of her'.[47]

There has also been speculation regarding Elizabeth Bennett, that 'she too had attracted attention in the village as a result of her lesbian relationship with Mrs Bonner.'[48] William Bonner was examined by Darcy on 24 February, revealing that Elizabeth Bennett and his wife were 'lovers and familiar friends' and spent much time together – a fact he seems to have somewhat resented.[49] His wife had been complaining of lameness in her knee, and he felt that Elizabeth Bennett was to blame for her condition worsening: by his account, Elizabeth had said, 'Ah good woman, how thou art loden,' before taking her in her arms and kissing her.[50] This led to his wife's lip swelling to an alarming size and her eyes sinking into her head, and she had been in the same sorry condition ever since. Despite the wording used it is likely that this has been interpreted through a modern understanding of words such as lover and kissing, and it is just as likely that William Bonner was driven to speak out against Elizabeth Bennett due to being unhappy with the perceived influence she had over his wife, rather than distaste for a sexual element to their relationship. It is also clear that Bonner was interviewed the same day that Ursula mentioned Elizabeth Bennett sending one of her spirits to plague Bonner's wife on the knee, and it therefore cannot be discounted that Bonner himself was called in to provide further 'proof' against her.

As with so much of the 'evidence' given in the St Osyth case, it is difficult to determine to what extent information given by witnesses was done so freely and how much was created by leading questions from Darcy, who already had an idea of the answers he was hoping to find. Familiarity with contemporary writings on demonology and witchcraft and the developing continental idea of the more sexual elements of witchcraft accusations may indeed have influenced what the justice was hoping to find, and led him to ask questions that would provide the required answers. It is equally likely that this was due to the fact that in the close-knit life of a sixteenth-century community, those who transgressed on sexual and moral grounds were unable to do so with impunity; offences were remembered, gossip ensured everyone knew what was going on with whom. At times of social unrest and heightened tensions, these things were brought up and those who were labelled were the most vulnerable and likely to be censured, the villagers of St Osyth unwittingly playing right into Darcy's hands by repeating the common knowledge about their neighbours.

The memory of the St Osyth trial and Ursula's fate have not faded over the centuries, with the events that took place and the individuals involved still remembered today if one knows where to look. One of the most poignant commemorations are the flowers left outside Colchester Castle to mark the injustices carried out at St Osyth, showing plainly that the individuals involved in witch trials there, both in 1582 and later under Matthew Hopkins, will never be forgotten.

Another location that holds strong connections to the St Osyth case is the Cage. Before being moved to Colchester Castle, it is believed that Ursula was first held there, the building being in those days the local lock-up in St Osyth. A plaque commemorates the fact, reading:

> The Cage
> Mediaeval Prison
> St Osyth Resident Ursula Kempe
> was imprisoned here before being
> hanged as a witch in 1582.

The Cage itself has a unique and turbulent history, and there are some that claim it is one of the most haunted houses in England. There are many who believe Ursula's spirit remains there to this day, unable to rest, forever in torment due to her unfair treatment over 400 years ago.[51]

It is rare indeed for the resting place of one executed for witchcraft to be known with any certainty, as most were buried away from the churchyards and, with no official burial, records are hard to come by. In 1921, the discovery of two reputedly female skeletons in the garden of a St Osyth house sparked great excitement, as they were quickly said to have been the remains of none other than Ursula Kempe and Elizabeth Bennett. The bodies were said to have been pinned to the ground with iron spikes in order to keep the spirit from escaping and causing further torment, and were buried in a north-south alignment.[52] Coupled with the fact that they were interred away from consecrated ground, the 'evidence' pointed towards witches and the remains soon became a local attraction, with the owner of the house capitalising on the fact, charging visitors to view the fascinating remains.[53] It may be said that Ursula disapproved of this exploitation, as a mysterious fire at the property brought such business to a sharp halt, and the skeletons were for a long while out of the limelight. In the 1960s, 'Ursula's' skeleton finally found a new home at the Museum of Witchcraft and Magic at Boscastle in Cornwall, purchased by Cecil Williamson, who then owned the museum. The bones remained there unmolested until purchased by artist and collector Robert Lenkiewicz, who eventually, with much prompting to follow through with his purchase, brought her to his rooms in Plymouth. Quite what Ursula made of this is unknown, but instances of the ill-treated witch making her presence known were recorded during her stay there, with varied reports of windows flying open or being jammed shut, alarms going off and other strange happenings taking place in the building where she was kept.

Does the skeleton really belong to one of England's most notorious witches? John Worland set out to prove the case once and for all, the result being the enlightening, well-researched and compelling DVD *Ursula Kemp: A Much Wronged Woman*.[54] Giving an outline of the St Osyth case and the history of the skeleton's discovery, the intriguing story is told in full for the first time, from discovery to eventual outcome as Worland strives to discover the identity of the body. In conclusion, although carbon dating and extensive examination revealed the bones to be sixteenth century in origin, the intriguing exploration of the evidence proves conclusively that the skeleton does not in fact belong to Ursula Kempe.[55] In 2012 the bones were finally laid to rest, the skeleton that was believed for so long to have been Ursula's returned to the ground from which it had come.[56] Just where Ursula really lies remains, for now, a mystery.

Chapter 2

Possession and Posturing:
The Witches of Warboys 1589–1593

...she had not been there long but the child grew something
worse than she was at her coming, and on the sudden cried,
saying 'Grandmother, look, where the old witch sitteth' –
pointing to the same Mother Samuel. 'Did you ever see' said
the child, 'one more like a witch than she is? Take off her
black thrummed cap, for I cannot abide to look on her.

The most strange and admirable discovery
of the three witches of Warboys, 1593

The idea of being possessed by a devil or devils was not a new one to
sixteenth-century England. Indeed, the fear was very real from biblical
times and beyond, developed and continued through the writings of scholars
and demonologists and popular opinion alike.

In the reign of Elizabeth I, the Throckmorton family – Robert and
Elizabeth Throckmorton, along with their seven surviving children –
were to experience the horrors of suspected possession first-hand, within
their own home.[1] The family were said to have been newcomers to the
Huntingdonshire village of Warboys when around 10 November 1589 their
daughter Jane, aged 9, was taken unwell with a sudden and inexplicable
illness.[2] The girl was tormented with sneezing fits that lasted up to half an
hour at a time, and also suffered fainting spells; whilst unconscious, Jane's
belly swelled so greatly she was nearly lifted from the bed, and no one could
bring her flat again. The girl also shook terribly, suffering from alarming fits
from which no one could rouse her.

As was to be expected, neighbours of the Throckmortons came to the
manor house to visit the ailing child and to share their sympathies with the
worried family. Amongst them was Alice Samuel, an elderly woman who
lived close by with her husband and daughter. Alice would come to deeply

regret her desire to be neighbourly, as when she took a seat close by the girl, Jane's condition suddenly worsened, and she shouted out:

> Grandmother, look where the old witch sitteth. Did you ever see one more like a witch than she is? Take off her black thrummed cap, for I cannot abide to look on her.[3]

As she spoke, Jane pointed at Alice Samuel, leaving no doubt as to whom she was referring. The girl's mother was also present and quick to rebuke her daughter for her outburst; a bed was quickly made up for Jane in the room, and attempts made to settle her as Alice Samuel looked on before finally leaving for her own home.

Two days later Jane was no better and the Throckmortons sent a sample of her urine to be examined by a physician. The doctor could find nothing wrong, other than that the girl might be suffering with worms, and accordingly he sent medicine to deal with that ailment. Jane did not improve, and two days later the now greatly troubled Throckmortons wrote to the doctor again, giving further details of their daughter's fits and intimating that they were concerned she might be afflicted with epilepsy. The doctor again replied that he could find nothing physically wrong, and was most certain that Jane was not epileptic. He did send further medicine, this time hoping that purging the girl would help bring some relief.

When the doctor wrote a few days later to enquire how his medicine was helping, the Throckmortons replied that it had not helped in the slightest and that their daughter was still suffering for all to see. Perplexed, as the urine showed no physical sign as to what ailed Jane, the doctor then made a suggestion that would have fatal consequences: did the parents suspect that Jane might have been bewitched?

Despite what later transpired, at this point the Throckmortons answered in the negative. Upon receiving this response the doctor repeated that he was out of ideas for a physical cause for Jane's suffering, but that they were more than welcome to consult with another doctor for a second opinion to put their minds at rest. This was duly done, but the next doctor was of the same opinion as the first; he suspected worms, though there was no sign of them in the urine, and he had to admit that the girl's symptoms didn't really support such a diagnosis. He even prescribed the same cure as the first doctor, which the parents did not bother to follow after the previous failed attempts.

Despite the Throckmortons dismissing the idea that witchcraft was behind their daughter's suffering, a month later something occurred that made them reconsider: Mary and Elizabeth Throckmorton, Jane's elder sisters, were taken ill in the same mysterious fashion. They too pointed the finger at Alice Samuel, begging for the old woman to be taken out of their presence, certain that if she was not removed she would kill them. This would have been alarming enough in itself, but to further muddy the waters, the old woman was not physically present at the time, reinforcing the idea that the girls were being tormented by supernatural means. It was not long before the youngest daughter, Grace, was likewise taken ill and by the end of January 1590, the eldest daughter, Joan, was also afflicted.

In their fits, the girls experienced several assaults upon their senses, and at different points they were found to be unable to hear, see or feel. The only thing they seemed consistently aware of was Alice Samuel, causing those who watched great distress as they shouted and pleaded for the old woman to be taken away from them. No help could be given, as Alice Samuel was noticeable to onlookers only for her absence in the Throckmorton household, where by this time she no doubt felt far from welcome.

Of the three suffering girls, 15-year-old Joan Throckmorton was stricken the worst of them all: the spirit, for that was what Robert and Elizabeth Throckmorton were now certain was assailing their children, 'forced her to sneeze, screech and groan very fearfully'.[4] Joan was also bounced and thrown around, both in her bed and when sitting in a chair, by unseen forces, a sight most terrible to behold for her horrified family.

As time went on, matters took an even stranger turn, as the 'spirit' itself started to communicate openly with and through Joan Throckmorton. It promised that it would tell her things, which she was then to tell others. The first prediction was that twelve people within the household would be bewitched: herself and her sisters, along with several maids. In due course several maids did indeed start to suffer in the same way as the girls, providing further proof that the household was bewitched and under attack from sinister forces. The suffering servants too called out against Alice Samuel, blaming her for what they were going through.

In February 1590, three months after the strange illness had first plagued the Throckmorton girls, their uncle, Gilbert Pickering, travelled to Warboys to visit the family.[5] Although the children appeared well enough when Pickering arrived, he was informed not long after that a group of neighbours were going to Alice Samuel's house to bring her to visit the girls in hope of putting right the situation. It was soon relayed that Alice was not inclined to submit to the request; having heard how the girls had accused her it is not surprising that she was reluctant to enter the house, especially as she had voiced a fear that the Throckmortons intended to have her 'scratched' in order to break the hold she was said to have over their daughters. Hearing of her refusal, Gilbert Pickering himself then went to try and persuade the old woman to undo whatever hold she had on his suffering nieces. When she still refused, Pickering got rather more heavy handed, informing Alice that he had the power to remove her from her house against her will. This threat was duly carried out, and Alice Samuel, along with her daughter Agnes and another woman, Cicely Burder, (both of whom were said to be witches and working with Alice), were duly escorted towards the manor house.[6]

On the walk to the Throckmorton house, Alice made several attempts to speak with her daughter, but was prevented from doing so by the suspicious Pickering. When they reached their destination Alice at last succeeded, apparently hissing to Agnes the incriminating words, 'I charge thee, do not confess anything!'[7] Pickering overheard this and chastised the woman, challenging her with what he had heard. Alice flatly denied everything, insisting that she had only been telling her daughter to hurry home to make dinner for her father.

As the party stepped into the house, three of the Throckmorton girls were in the hall. Although they had been well moments before, as Alice Samuel appeared the girls were immediately thrown into fits once more, twisting and turning in a tormented fashion that left onlookers aghast. Jane, the girl with whom the entire situation had started, was carried into anther room where attempts where made to calm her, but with little success. Following, Gilbert Pickering observed the girl scratching at the bed-covers, repeating the words: 'Oh, that I had her! Oh, that I had her!'[8] When Pickering put his own hand within reach of Jane's, the girl refused to scratch it, pushing it away and scratching again at the bed.[9] Pickering was quick then to fetch Alice, bringing her, with great reluctance on Alice's part, to Jane's side. When instructed to place her hand close to Jane's, Alice refused, leading Pickering to take her hand and to force it there. Although the girl had not scratched his own hand or that of others who had put theirs close by, upon sensing Alice's hand Jane reacted violently, scratching Alice with such force that it broke the girl's nails. As if this were not evidence enough for those gathered there, Gilbert Pickering then put his hand in the way of Alice's; the moment he did so, Jane stopped scratching, resuming her frantic search for the hand she wanted. This and various other tests were carried out, until it was seen without a doubt that Jane would scratch Alice's hand and no other.[10]

After witnessing this and more during his brief visit, Gilbert Pickering returned home the next day to his native Titchmarsh, taking with him the second eldest Throckmorton daughter, Elizabeth. This was perhaps an attempt to bring her and her family some respite from suffering, or, more likely, to more closely witness the strange behaviour that he had seen in his nieces.[11] Intriguingly, the moment Elizabeth was away from the manor hose, she recovered from the fit she had been suffering. The respite proved short-lived: upon arrival she once again became sorely afflicted.

Continuing a theme from home, at dinner times during her stay, Elizabeth grew increasingly agitated when it came time for prayers, falling into a fit accordingly. Furthermore, reading out loud from the Bible also threw the girl into torment, as she raged and writhed, only to fall silent again when the reader ceased. These behaviours continued throughout her visit, with the girl not even permitted to pray silently to God without being tormented in the same fashion. Dinner time was a particularly wretched affair for Elizabeth, as the spirit seemed to take delight in tormenting her, 'putting her hand besides her meat, and her meat besides her mouth, mocking her and making her miss her mouth'.[12]

An experiment that had been carried out at the Throckmorton household was also repeated; Elizabeth was carried from the house into the churchyard to see whether she recovered or stayed in her fits. Sure enough, upon leaving the house the girl was well, only to fall ill once more when she was returned indoors.[13] Despite being absent from home, it seemed Elizabeth maintained a connection with her sisters as, when they suffered something in Warboys, Elizabeth experienced the same at Titchmarsh Grove, and vice versa, further reinforcing the belief that witchcraft and spirits were to blame.

A month or so after Elizabeth Throckmorton went to stay with Gilbert Pickering, the Throckmorton household saw the arrival of further visitors: Lady Susan Cromwell (wife to Sir Henry Cromwell and posthumous step-grandmother to the infamous Oliver Cromwell), and her daughter-in-law, Mistress Cromwell. The women, friends of the family, came to see the suffering children and to offer what comfort they could to the unhappy parents. Soon after their arrival they were able to see first-hand the fits suffered by the children and, greatly upset by what she witnessed, Lady Cromwell sent for Alice Samuel.[14] Far from improving matters, with Alice's arrival the state of the children worsened further, and Lady Cromwell spoke sternly to Alice, accusing her of being the orchestrator of their suffering through her witchcraft. Alice denied the accusation, in her turn speaking against the Throckmortons for their dubious treatment of her. Lady Cromwell was not swayed by Alice's words, instead pointing out that it was the girls who had accused her, not their parents, and therefore Alice had no grounds for complaint.

As this conversation was taking place, Joan Throckmorton piped up, also insisting that Alice Samuel was to blame for her suffering and that 'someone' was currently telling her so. No one else could hear the voice, but the girl insisted that it 'squealed very loud in her ears', showing amazement that she was the only one to hear it.[15] Despite this, Alice Samuel again denied having any part in the matter, and strongly resisted the attempts of Lady Cromwell and a visiting doctor of divinity to take her upstairs for further questioning. Finally Lady Cromwell, realising she was getting nowhere, conceded defeat. Before Alice could escape however, she pulled off the 'kerchief' that covered Alice's head, cutting a piece of hair off with some shears.[16] The hair was then given to the mother of the children, with Lady Cromwell instructing her to burn it in the fire along with Alice's hair lace. Understandably aggrieved at being treated in this way, Alice Samuel demanded of Lady Cromwell, 'Madam, why do you use me thus? I never did you any harm as yet.'[17] These were perhaps the very worst words the accused woman could utter, as they were to be later remembered and used against her with fatal consequences.

The Cromwell women left the Throckmorton household that same day, but that night Lady Cromwell's dreams were plagued by Alice Samuel. Not in her own form, but in that of a cat, which Lady Cromwell thought the old woman had sent to her. This cat, said Lady Cromwell, threatened to remove the skin from her body, the horrors of the dream causing her to writhe about and cry out so much that she woke Mistress Cromwell who was sharing her bed. The younger woman woke Lady Cromwell, who then proceeded to tell her all about the nightmare, so terrified by the experience that she could not sleep again that night. Not only that, Lady Cromwell fell 'strangely sick' soon after, and finally died of her mysterious ailment – that was said to be similar to that suffered by the Throckmorton girls – a year and a quarter after her encounter with Alice Samuel, never forgetting until her dying day the words the suspected witch had spoken to her.[18]

Meanwhile, the Throckmorton girls continued in their sorry state until Christmas 1590 came around. Henry Pickering, another uncle to the girls, went to stay with the family during the festive season, and was likewise deeply vexed by what he observed there. During his stay of around four days, Henry Pickering decided that he too wanted to speak with Alice Samuel, asking two scholars of his acquaintance to accompany him. The three men made their way to confront Alice about her part in the illness that was plaguing the Throckmorton family, although, so the account stresses, without the knowledge of Master and Mistress Throckmorton or the girls in question. Alice herself happened to be leaving her house as the group approached, and the men decided to follow her in order to evade the notice of John Samuel, who, they surmised, would not look kindly on them accosting his wife. Accordingly, they followed Alice on her errand to a neighbour, waiting until she was finished before trying to speak with her. Alice was again reluctant to talk, refusing to answer the questions that were put to her. She was more forthcoming regarding her thoughts on the Throckmortons, both parents and children, railing against how badly they had used her, and how she did not understand why they were treating her so. She also declared her belief that the girls were faking their symptoms, and that they would not get away with such behaviour if they were *her* children.

Alice was then questioned about her relationship with God, but again she would not be drawn, insisting only that 'her' God would not see her suffer. Henry Pickering and his companions leapt upon this choice of phrasing, asking quickly if Alice did not worship the same God as they did. Alice insisted that she did, but did not change her wording, deepening their suspicions further. Unable to get any more out of the old woman, they were preparing to leave when Henry Pickering's feelings got the better of him; he told Alice that if she were indeed responsible for the suffering of his nieces then God would surely punish her, however much she continued to deny it. Indeed, the only way to avoid such a fate was to confess and repent, 'which if she did not in time, he hoped one day to see her burned at a stake, and he himself would bring fire and wood, and the children should blow the coals.'[19] Alice replied heatedly and, as she showed no sign of confessing anything or being swayed by his words, they went their separate ways amidst much anger on both sides.

Much to Alice's detriment, it transpired that at the same time as this interview was taking place, Joan Throckmorton was suffering a fit at home. With apparently no foreknowledge of the whereabouts of her uncle, she declared that Henry Pickering and two men had gone to see Alice Samuel. Not only that, but the girl seemed to have an uncanny knowledge of what was going on, relating accurately to those with her the events that were taking place. Hearing this, Robert Throckmorton made enquires as to the whereabouts of Henry Pickering (for it seems, if the story be believed, that Henry had left without telling anyone his intentions – again conveniently relieving the Throckmortons from any direct involvement against Alice), but no one could tell him. Thinking there might be some truth in his daughter's pronouncements, Master Throckmorton then went out to find Pickering, meeting the party on their return. When asked where he had been, Henry Pickering related events, his story identical to what Joan had told her father before he had left the house.

As the months passed and with the 'evidence' stacking up against Alice, the girls continued to accuse the old woman of tormenting them with spirits that did her bidding. One of these often came in the guise of a chicken; it would not only tell the girls of Alice's intention to harm them, but also acted as an eavesdropper on their enemy, telling them everything that Alice did throughout the day whilst she was in her own house and out of their sight.[20]

The spirit also proved itself most cunning; telling the girls that Alice was to blame for their suffering, it also pointed out that if they were taken to the Samuel house, they would feel better. Duly, this test was carried out on several occasions; each time the girls miraculously recovered, coming to themselves to express utter bewilderment as to why they were at Alice's house, and remembering nothing of what had taken place in their fits. The relief was short-lived, as the moment the girls were taken back to their own home, they returned to their formerly wretched states. It was also observed that on the rare occasions that Alice Samuel could be persuaded to go to the Throckmorton household, the girls would also recover from their fits, only to lapse back into them again as soon as she had left.

1592 drew round and the Throckmorton family had been suffering now for over two years. All those who witnessed the terrible state of the girls were greatly upset by what they saw, and friends and family alike were growing desperate to do anything they could to improve the situation. Indeed, the only thing that seemed to cause any improvement whatsoever was the presence of Alice Samuel. Desperate and at his wits' end, it was then that Robert Throckmorton decided that he would secure the relief of his daughters at whatever cost.

No longer willing to equivocate, the determined father approached John Samuel with a proposition: Robert Throckmorton announced that he would pay the equivalent amount for the most well-paid servant in the area, in return for John Samuel allowing his wife to live at the manor house. Known for being decidedly surly, Alice's husband refused the offer, but Robert Throckmorton would not be dissuaded. As Alice would not come to him, he decided to take the children to Alice, bringing them to the Samuel household where he threatened to leave them so that they might be well. John Samuel in turn doused the fire and declared that he would starve the girls, his own daughter, Agnes, also piping up in cross response against Robert Throckmorton. This had no effect, and the girls remained in the house all that day, showing no sign of the fits that had plagued them for so long in their own home. As night fell and they showed no sign of leaving, John Samuel, by this time keen to be rid of his unwanted guests, made the promise that if they left, the next day he would send Alice to their house as Robert Throckmorton had previously asked. The sisters duly departed – falling ill once more as they returned home – and, according to the account, spent a most terrible night suffering in their own beds.

Furthermore, there was trickery afoot, as when Master Throckmorton went to collect Alice Samuel the next morning, she was nowhere to be found. In response, Throckmorton once again set up camp in the Samuel household with his daughters, remaining until evening when Alice finally returned home. Upon seeing them, Alice confessed that she had been away out of town and that her husband had told her to make herself absent in order not to make good the promise to go with Robert Throckmorton. Such honesty on Alice's part did her no favours, as John Samuel hotly denied everything and in his anger, beat his wife with a cudgel before she could be dragged to safety.

Eventually, Robert Throckmorton got his way; when John Samuel realised that the other man was not going to back down, he finally agreed that Alice could go with him as previously promised. Alice, having no say in the matter herself, was therefore taken to the manor house, where a seemingly miraculous occurrence took place. The girls were all well and together, the first time they had been so in over a year.

Throckmorton and his wife were, understandably, hugely relieved at this, and, if the account is to be believed, Alice Samuel was treated as an honoured guest within the household. However, ten days into her stay, when Alice asked if she might return home to fetch something she required, Mistress Throckmorton equivocated, offering to go instead to fetch the item. Alice insisted that she go and was granted permission to return home briefly. She had not been out of the house for long when the girls began to suffer once more, being told by one of the spirits that Alice had gone home to feed the others that did her bidding. Worse, the spirit continued, Alice was in the process of striking a new bargain which would have dire consequences for the Throckmorton children; whereas before the girls were well when Alice was at their house, now, due to the new arrangement, they would suffer all the more when in her presence.

As far-fetched as this seemed, the tale did appear to be borne out by events when Alice returned a few hours later. The usual relief experienced by the children at her presence in the house was noticeably absent, and they continued to suffer, a fact that greatly vexed their increasingly desperate parents. Furthermore, the girls insisted that Alice was feeding her spirits whilst in their house, and when Alice denied this they claimed that one of the spirits told them differently; that Alice could not only see and hear the spirit, but had sent it to them as well.

Alice continued to deny any knowledge of such spirits, but irrefutable 'proof' was obtained some time later. One day, a Throckmorton cousin also staying in the household alerted Robert Throckmorton to the fact that Alice Samuel's chin was bleeding. When he went to see, it was clear that the cousin spoke the truth, drops of blood visible on Alice's chin despite her attempts to hide the fact with a napkin. Not only that, but on closer examination, older small red marks were also discovered, taken as evidence that she had been feeding the spirits undetected for some time. Cornered, Alice admitted at last that her chin bled often, but insisted it was from a perfectly innocent cause, although she could not explain what this was to the satisfaction of her questioners.

The spirits, whether sent by Alice or not, were certainly ruling the Throckmorton household. Neither were they content with bad-mouthing just Alice; Agnes and John Samuel soon came under fire as well. On one occasion the spirits told Robert Throckmorton that if they went to the Samuel household, Agnes would hide away and pretend not to be at home. To test this pronouncement, Master Throckmorton made his way there, and indeed John Samuel said his daughter was not at home and that he did not know where she was. Throckmorton pressed, and asked whether Agnes was in the room above them, as he had his suspicions as to her whereabouts, but again John Samuel said he didn't know – a response belied by the fact that the stairs to the upstairs chamber were close to the foot of his bed, where the man had been reposing before the knock at the door. Suspecting full well where Agnes was, Master Throckmorton called her name several times, but the girl still remained silent. It was only when he threatened to fetch an iron bar in order to enter the room that Agnes finally called down to confess her presence. Master Throckmorton left with the knowledge that John Samuel and Agnes had lied and that the spirits had again, it seemed, spoken the truth.

As the weeks dragged on, even the decidedly Throckmorton-biased account of events relates how Alice was fed up with being – in all but name – a prisoner at the manor house. The girls continued to report everything she did or said to anyone who would listen, and the old woman could not move without everyone knowing of her actions. It seemed that the end was finally coming; the girls, through the prompting of the spirits, took on a new mantra. Alice would confess her guilt 'before the Tuesday after Twelfth day' – that was, the Tuesday after 6 January.[21] This was to be a day of great joy as, by confessing, Alice would ensure that the girls were made well again. Furthermore, if Alice confessed *before* the given date, recovery would come all the sooner; with this in mind, the Throckmorton daughters continually beseeched Alice to confess and put them out of their misery.

Alice's response to this hectoring was that she would not confess to something she had not done; the girls agreed they would not want her to do so, but at the same time insisted that they said only what the spirits had told them, and that they believed Alice was indeed responsible for their suffering. Through the spirits the girls also spoke at length about the depravity of Alice's life: her haphazard church attendance, her use of bad language, her bad words against the Throckmorton family when they displeased her, and having raised her own daughter to be as lewd as she was.

Faced with such unrelenting criticism, Alice, according to the account, confessed that all of this was true in regards to her life, although she still would not admit to having bewitched them. She also promised the children that she would mend her wicked ways from that point on and live a more virtuous life. Emboldened, the girls also took Alice to task on her previous assertion that they were faking their fits; when pressed, Alice agreed that she no longer thought this, another triumph for the Throckmorton sisters. Gracious in victory, the girls said they would pray with everything in them that Alice would confess, and that if she did, they would forgive her and encourage everyone else to do so in thanks that they were free at last from the torment of the last few years.

As moving as such a display might have been to those who observed it – many, it was said, were moved to tears – as Christmas approached, Alice remained singularly resistant to the final and pressing point of a confession to bewitching the girls. One thing even the pamphlet author could not avoid mentioning was how Alice herself suffered during this time; it was said that she had a nosebleed nearly every day and not only that, looked pale and close to fainting. As the day of Alice's predicted confession drew nearer, the old woman's physical complaints steadily worsened. Her back hurt, as did her stomach; some days it was her knee, and others she was in such pain that she could not rest at all. One night she was in such distress that she woke Master Throckmorton and his wife who were sleeping near her. When they asked what was wrong Alice said that the pain was in her belly and something was in it, she had felt it stir and it was the size of a penny loaf. When examined by Mistress Throckmorton, a mass or swelling of the size described was indeed found, though no further examination took place as the night was cold and the other woman soon retreated back to her own bed. In her anguish, Alice called out to the Throckmortons that she was in great pain. The evil spirits that plagued the household were responsible both for the suffering of the children and also her own current misery she declared, one of them being in her stomach and causing her pain; she wished, she said, that she had never gone there. Robert Throckmoton's response was less than sympathetic; if there were evil spirits in the household, he reasoned, they were there at her bidding. Alice spent the remainder of the night in great agony, and in the morning she was no better, even though the outward swelling was gone.[22]

Despite her obvious suffering, the spirits – and the girls who acted as their mouthpiece – showed no mercy. As the pressure for Alice to confess on or before the appointed date mounted, Jane Throckmorton upped the stakes, falling into such a great fit that her very life was considered to be in danger. Alice, no doubt desperate by this time, prayed earnestly for the girl to recover, but the more she prayed the more the child suffered, especially if the names of God or Jesus were uttered. The spirit assured Jane that there was worse to come; shortly before she was finally released from the fit she was told that she was, in the near future, to suffer a fit of greater magnitude than she had ever yet experienced. Even this news could not drag a confession from Alice; despite Jane's sisters begging her to speak so that they could have a happy Christmas, Alice could only promise that although she would do anything she could to help them, she could not confess to something she had not done.

The net was closing in. When asked directly about this fit that Jane would suffer, Alice expressed the belief that with God's help the girl would not need to suffer it after all. Hearing this, Robert Throckmorton pressed further, suggesting that Alice might tell the spirit in the name of God not to make Jane suffer the fit that was said to be coming. Alice did so, and Jane told those gathered that the spirit had confirmed that, because of Alice's words, she would be spared from having the predicted fit. With this seeming success, Master Throckmorton told Alice to speak again and that this time she should pronounce that *none* of the girls would suffer again and would be well from then on. Alice complied, and the result was immediate; three of the girls had been in a fit for the last three weeks, but at Alice's words they instantly recovered, looking quite well and like their old selves.

Rather than being relieved, Alice responded with horror. She fell to her knees and pleaded forgiveness, much to the confusion of Robert Throckmorton who asked her what the matter was. Despite her previous denials, Alice told him then that she had been the cause of the trouble all along. When questioned further, she admitted that she had no reason to have done so, that the Throckmortons had given her no cause whatsoever to treat them in such a fashion, before again begging Robert Throckmorton's forgiveness. The relieved father was quick to give it, as Alice lamented that she had 'forsaken my maker and given my soul to the Devil'.[23]

Mistress Throckmorton and the children's grandmother shortly entered and Alice likewise begged their forgiveness, which was given, although the two women did not know yet what had transpired. Francis Dorington, the minister of Warboys and uncle to the children, was then sent for, and a great deal of time and effort went into attempts to calm the distraught Alice. They were only partially successful, and in church the next day Dorington, still under the guise of comforting Alice, informed the gathered congregation of everything she had confessed, his sermon and readings aimed at those with penitent hearts. Whatever his words they were clearly not soothing to the poor woman, and Alice cried and wailed her way through the service, unable to find solace in what was being said for her benefit.

Despite his apparent sympathy for the old woman, Robert Throckmorton couldn't help recalling that Alice had been untruthful with them before and gone back on her word on more than one occasion. She had only confessed before himself and his household, and, fearing this would not be enough, he asked for Alice to stand up in church and declare the truth of the matter before everyone assembled there. Throckmorton also insisted that she tell her listeners that she had confessed freely and without pressure: Alice did so, assuring the congregation that she had confessed of her own volition to bewitching the children.

After such turmoil, it was decided that Alice likewise needed to be reconciled with her husband. On Christmas Eve 1592 she returned home, her captivity at the manor house finally at an end. Far from being pleased to see Alice, John Samuel and their daughter Agnes were quick to express their displeasure at her having confessed; they harangued her so much that by the next day, Christmas Day itself, Alice had made a complete turnaround and denied everything she had admitted to the day before.

When Robert Throckmorton heard of this he and Francis Dorington were quick to visit the Samuel household. It just so happened that the family were discussing the very matter at the time of their arrival and, rather than knocking, the unexpected visitors eavesdropped at the window. Agnes Samuel was warning her parents not to believe anything 'they' – assumed by the narrator to be the Throckmortons and their supporters – had to say, counselling them on the necessity to keep from saying anything further. Throckmorton and his companion had heard enough; they entered the house a moment later, taking Agnes to task regarding her words, which she was quick to deny. Undeterred, they then turned on Alice herself, expressing their displeasure at her retraction and threatening to not only bring her before a justice to settle the matter but also to revoke the previous offer of favour and forgiveness now she had again used them so badly.[24] Despite this, Alice would not be moved, and further attempts the following day to make the old woman restate her confession proved fruitless; Alice insisted that she had confessed solely out of joy that the Throckmorton children were well again and nothing more.

With no other recourse, Robert Throckmorton made good his threat. Having sent for the constables to arrest Alice, he informed her that she would be taken to the Bishop of Lincoln and should prepare herself accordingly. No doubt freshly fearful at this turn of events, Alice drew Throckmorton aside, telling him now that she would confess again if only they were alone. Throckmorton took Alice into the parlour, where she proceeded to confess in the same manner as she had done previously. When a perplexed Throckmorton asked her to explain why, if this was the case, she had been so adamant in denying it, Alice admitted it was because of her husband and daughter. They had scolded her severely for confessing, and had warned her that everyone would now call her a witch for the rest of her life, something she was keen to avoid. At this, Throckmorton promised Alice favour once more, and when Francis Dorington conveniently appeared a short time afterwards, they wasted no time in making sure that the confession was committed to paper.

Determined that Alice would not escape again, Robert Throckmorton took the opportunity to hurry to the nearby church. Gathering several of the congregation there, he brought them back to the manor house, urging them to stand beneath the window of the room where Alice was repeating her confession to Dorington. Knowing full well what was taking place, Dorington encouraged Alice to speak louder, ostensibly for his own benefit, but in reality so that those listening would have no trouble hearing her words. Blissfully unaware, Alice did just that, only to be met, once she had finished, by the group of neighbours in the hall. When Dorington read out the freshly transcribed confession to those assembled, Alice tried to deny it once more, but there was no hope this time. They had all heard the confession from her own lips, and another recantation would not be accepted by anyone.

Amidst the confusion, John Samuel arrived, to be informed by a triumphant Throckmorton that his wife had again confessed and the only reason for Alice's previous denial had been her fear of him. The angry husband demanded of Alice whether this were true, before launching himself at her in a violent attack. Those gathered moved to hold him back but Alice effectively saved herself, falling into a faint.[25]

Alice was duly examined before the Bishop of Lincoln on 26 December, 1592 and again on the twenty-ninth of that month.[26] In the first examination, Alice was asked the decidedly leading question of whether a dun chicken had ever sucked her chin. Alice gave the somewhat evasive reply that it had sucked her only twice since last Christmas Eve. In another question designed to get the required answer, Alice was then asked whether the chicken involved was of a 'natural' sort. She confessed that it wasn't, as it seemed to feed from her without causing discomfort or without her being really aware of it; it was only when she brushed it away with her hand and found blood there that she knew what had happened. The chicken had visited her before she went to the Throckmorton household, Alice said, and the suffering of the Throckmorton children had been the fault of the chicken; it was, however, now gone from her.

The second examination three days later was longer, and began with Alice stressing that the only people to whom she had caused harm were the Throckmorton children. When asked how she was certain that the chicken was no longer present to torment the children Alice replied that she knew because both the chicken and the other spirits were now inside her belly, making her 'so full that she is like to burst'.[27]

In her examinations, Alice also mentioned the 'upright man' from whom she had first received the spirits, who she had finally learned was named Langland. This man had gone on 'the last voyage beyond the seas.'[28] The names of the spirits who had done her bidding were also confirmed as Pluck, Catch, White, and three that, confusingly, went by the name of Smack. She had initially sent them to Throckmorton and his wife, but they had been unable to do anything to the devout couple, and so she had moved instead to the children, the success of which could be all too readily testified.

After Alice's examinations she and her daughter were taken to the gaol in Huntingdon, the daughter also under suspicion it seemed. Agnes Samuel remained in prison with her mother until 9 January, when Robert Throckmorton requested that the young woman be released on bail and allowed to come to his home so they could determine whether she too was guilty of the crimes against his family. After some persuasion this permission was reluctantly granted by those in authority, and as her mother had been before her, Agnes herself became an unwilling guest at the manor house of Warboys.[29] Any relief she might have felt at her release must have been short-lived; the spirits, still talking through the Throckmorton girls, announced not long after her arrival that Agnes had bewitched the girls afresh after they had been freed by Alice, as the mother had passed her spirits on to her daughter. Agnes was thus subjected to the same treatment as her mother; her movements throughout the house were reported on and predicted by the spirits, and nothing she did went unnoticed. Agnes was also made to repeat words that would free the girls from their renewed sufferings; in an elaborate display, she was made first to charge the spirits with leaving in the name of God, saying: 'I charge thee, Devil, in the name of the God of heaven and earth, as I hate thee and am no witch, nor guilty of this matter, that thou depart from this child and suffer her to come forth of her fit.'[30] Nothing happened. Next, Agnes was instructed to say the same formula, but this time in the name of *being* a witch: the Throckmorton girl was, after that, seemingly made well, something that was taken to prove Agnes's guilt. To make matters even worse, the wording was further honed to include the words: 'As I am a witch and consenting to the death of the Lady Cromwell,' the death of whom was ultimately to be laid at the door of the Samuel women.[31]

Whilst Agnes was in the household, Mary Throckmorton was talking with the spirit during a fit and asked it to confirm if she would scratch the 'young witch' (as she called Agnes) on that day. Hearing this, her uncle took Agnes to Mary's side, where the girl proceeded to accuse Agnes of being the cause of all of her suffering. The shocked young woman was then instructed to carry Mary downstairs, but when Agnes picked her up, Mary attacked her, scratching her violently. This was no small thing; the distressed and crying Agnes could not shake off the girl, and Mary succeeded in scratching skin from her face 'the breadth of a shilling'.[32] Mary's words were equally distressing and violent, as the girl declared that 'I will scratch you, you young witch, and pay you home for this punishing of me and my sisters!'[33]

No one moved to help the distressed Agnes, but the crying young woman was finally able to carry Mary downstairs as instructed. Despite the violence of the attack, only water appeared on Agnes's face, the expected blood chillingly absent, this fact taken as yet further proof of witchcraft. When Mary came out of her fit the girl seemed very remorseful for what she had done, insisting that she had only attacked Agnes because the spirit had ordered her to. Mary was not the only sister to scratch Agnes during her stay, and she was attacked at several points during her time with the Throckmortons. On 2 April, Joan Throckmorton finally got her chance to carry out the threat she had made on 19 March when she had predicted she would herself scratch Agnes. Joan got her in a headlock and scratched her right cheek and then the left, declaring of the latter that it was done for her Aunt Pickering whom it was believed Alice and Agnes had made ill.[34]

Therefore, despite having scolded her mother for doing what the Throckmortons wanted, Agnes herself had done just that; not only saying words that would eventually condemn her, but – understandably given her vulnerable position – allowing the girls to scratch her and treat her as they did. John Samuel was another matter, and he refused to play into what he saw all too well as an elaborate and deadly charade. Although Joan Throckmoton spoke out against him in his presence for his wicked ways, John Samuel remained unimpressed, speaking over the girl and telling her that she was wicked and her words pure invention.[35] Alice's husband then returned to his home, leaving the other Throckmorton girls to follow their sister's example in making accusations against him.

Meanwhile, during her time in gaol, Alice's situation went from bad to worse. First, one of the gaoler's servants died, for which the old woman was blamed. Second, it was said that Alice had made one of the gaoler's children severely ill after the child had scratched her. Other incidents occurred that were seen as being caused by Alice's witchcraft and, the account insists, they were enough on their own to charge Alice as guilty – even without taking the enormity of her crimes against the Throckmorton children into consideration.

As the days went on, the impending case drew a great deal of attention, and by the time of the Assizes at Huntingdon on 4 April, 500 men came to see Joan Throckmorton in her fits. The girl had been lodged at the Crown Inn, and Agnes likewise was brought to join her. The purpose of this was soon made clear; when the visitors tried and failed to cure the sick girl, Agnes was brought forward to repeat the by now well-known formula, stopping the fits instantly much to the amazement of the onlookers. Later that day, the Judge himself came to show a group of gentlemen and fellow justices that the only way for the fits to be stopped was by Agnes, and the display did not disappoint.

That same day, Jane Throckmorton had likewise been publicly cured by the previously reluctant John Samuel. Despite his refusals to repeat the words that were said to be able to cure the girls, in court he was told that if he did not utter them he would immediately be sentenced to death. Faced with such a choice, John Samuel finally capitulated, saying: 'As I am a witch and did consent to the death of the Lady Cromwell, so I charge the devil to suffer Mistress Jane to come out of her fit at this present.'[36] As expected by all concerned, Jane was immediately and visibly well, bringing the third member of the Samuel family to finally 'admit' his guilt.

The following day, Alice, Agnes and John Samuel were indicted by the court with the bewitching to death of Lady Cromwell, and also for bewitching Joan and Jane Throckmorton, both of which were punishable crimes under the 1563 Witchcraft Act. It took five hours for the witnesses to give their evidence against the family, with others, including the gaoler, coming forward to name their grievances and the terrible crimes of the Samuels. All three were duly found guilty and sentenced to death.[37]

At the verdict, Alice Samuel attempted to make use of the only recourse available to her – pleading pregnancy as a means to escape the noose.[38] Given her age, those present in court found the very suggestion preposterously funny, but despite their laughter Alice insisted. She was duly examined by a group of women appointed for the purpose, only for them to report that she was not, after all, with child and therefore fit to meet with the fate the court had dealt her. When the considerably younger Agnes was likewise prompted by someone to try the same ruse, the unmarried woman refused, declaring proudly that she would not be known as a whore as well as a witch.

The execution took place Friday 5 April, on Mill Common, a mere ten minute walk from the gaol where the Samuels spent their final night. There were about forty people present to witness their end.[39]

Perhaps one of the greatest indignities and torments in a long line of both in the whole sorry affair was that suffered by Alice Samuel as she came to the scaffold. If the report is taken to be correct, she was quizzed in the moments before death by a Doctor Chamberlain, who, in front of the assembled crowd, asked Alice for the names of her spirits and whether she had bewitched Lady Cromwell and the Throckmorton daughters. Facing the end of her life, Alice was then made to relate which spirits had done these deeds, and various details as to the when and where and how, though, as is noticeably lacking throughout, she was never asked the pressing question of *why*. When asked if her husband was a witch Alice said he was, but refused to incriminate Agnes in any way, maintaining to the very end that her daughter was innocent. There was still to be no respite for the suffering woman, as Alice was further hounded into reciting the Lord's Prayer and the Creed.[40] Alice was finally, and perhaps by this point, thankfully, released from such questioning, her life, and that of her husband and daughter ending a short while later.

Even after death Alice was not left in peace. When her body was examined for further proof of the witchcraft she had died for, a teat was discovered close to her private parts, which, when squeezed, produced liquid, then milk, and then finally blood. This was, those who witnessed the sight were sure, the final proof that the accusations against Alice and her family were just and that the reign of terror of a witch was at an end.[41]

****

In the Warboys Parish registers, there is no trace of the family of Alice and John Samuel so it is impossible to know with any certainty how long they had lived in Warboys, their ages, that of their daughter Agnes, or if they had any further children or close family in the village.[42]

Even so, the question must also be posed as to why the Samuels were disliked enough within the community of Warboys that no one came to their aid or spoke for them at any point during their troubles with the Throckmorton family. John Samuel's reputation for violence has already been mentioned, and the fact that he was considered an unpleasant sort is easily discernible from the words used of him in the account.[43] Alice herself was referred to as loud of voice and harsh in manner, both seen as unwomanly and undesirable qualities, and common complaints against those accused of witchcraft during the period.[44] It is therefore entirely possible that Alice was not well liked within the village, and that her husband's abrasiveness and violent ways made them vulnerable within the close-knit nature of a sixteenth-century village community. It is also therefore highly possible that the Throckmorton girls had heard rumours regarding the family and played into this, either consciously or subconsciously, when targeting Alice as the cause of their suffering. Interestingly, Alice confessed to her 'lewd' life as painted by the Throckmorton girls, suggesting she considered this herself to be a just accusation. In light of this, it is equally intriguing that she continued at that time to maintain her innocence where the spirits were concerned. Alice's potentially bad reputation within Warboys and beyond could certainly explain why no one came to help her, making it all the easier for the campaign of persecution against the older woman to be carried out.

One thing that *is* clear from the account is that Alice also endured physical and emotional abuse from her husband, John Samuel's attacks against his wife noted on several occasions throughout the relating of events. Sadly, domestic violence was again not uncommon in the Samuels' strata of society, and a wife in such a position as Alice found herself with very little recourse or ability to protect herself.[45]

To a modern reader, the treatment Alice Samuel experienced at the hands of those who accused her of bewitching the Throckmorton daughters is chilling and distressing in equal measure. Even though the only surviving contemporary account of events is clearly written in the favour of the Throckmorton family, it is impossible to fully disguise the fact that the elderly and economically dependent Alice Samuel was, to all intents, hounded, abused and finally held prisoner by the more prestigious and well-connected family.[46] Her daughter Agnes experienced the same treatment to a lesser degree, reflecting the harsh reality and helplessness of such women against their social and economic superiors. Indeed, the whole pamphlet that relates events can be taken as an after-the-fact effort to absolve the Throckmortons of any culpability in the entire affair, the author clearly biased in favour of the victors. In view of this, the number of times the biased narrators are unable to conceal the fact that Alice Samuel was horribly mistreated is damning.

The intention to distance the Throckmortons from blame is a clear theme throughout the account, beginning with the assertion that Robert and Elizabeth Throckmorton did not at first suspect witchcraft when Jane fell ill towards the end of 1589. Although the author does, it must be said, labour the point too much to be entirely convincing, this does in fact hold true with evidence from other similar cases. People did not immediately leap to the assumption that they or their family had been bewitched when illness or other symptoms presented themselves, and, as in the case of the Throckmortons, it was only after conventional medicine had proved wanting that other, alternative, explanations and cures were sought.

There is less room for denial over the treatment Alice received. Although the author of the pamphlet is at great pains to stress that the Throckmortons treated Alice with much care during her stay with them, and that Alice owed Robert Throckmorton much due to the kindnesses she received, the assertion rings somewhat hollow. Despite being expected to do nothing apart from the work she set herself, and that she was also fed as well as the rest of the family, the fact that Alice was, and remained, a virtual prisoner in the household cannot be avoided. Furthermore, when Elizabeth Throckmorton found herself unable to eat or drink during mealtimes as willed by Alice's 'spirit', the decision was made that until Elizabeth could eat again, Alice could not eat either, a chilling hint of the lengths the Throckmortons would go to in order to control her.

To what extent the final, terrible outcome was planned in any way by the Throckmortons can only be speculated at; although by the point Alice finally confessed and was promised favour by Robert Throckmorton it does seem that he was determined, despite his words, to see justice done, and played Alice accordingly.[47]

One must perhaps spare some sympathy for Robert and Elizabeth Throckmorton – at least initially. If the account is to be believed, they were faced with the eventual suffering of all of their daughters, whilst being powerless to do anything to help them. Medicine had not helped, nor had prayer. For the sixteenth-century parent there were precious few remaining avenues left available to explore, and the helplessness they must have felt if they fully believed their daughters to be so tormented can only be imagined, especially given the long duration and increasing severity of their conditions. This does not excuse their hounding of Alice Samuel in any way, but does go a little way to perhaps understanding their intentions and actions.

The most pressing question of the whole affair and one that has perplexed readers across the centuries is what exactly was behind the actions of the girls? The fits and strange symptoms they seemed to suffer went on for a staggering period of three-and-a-half years and were believed to be genuine by all, or nearly all, of the people who witnessed their suffering.[48]

The first point to consider is whether the girls were in fact genuinely suffering from some sort of physical ailment, despite the doctors consulted by the family being unable to offer a plausible medical explanation for the girls' illness. It has been suggested that physical symptoms such as weakness, muscle pain and skin changes point to a real illness or disorder; vitamin deficiency caused by poor diet, or the proximity of Warboys to the wet and damp fenland could explain at least some of what was witnessed in the Throckmorton children and the others in the household who claimed to have been bewitched by Alice Samuel.[49]

The Throckmortons clearly believed their children to be possessed, and such a belief was not new or exclusive to the Warboys story. Possession, the taking over of the victim by a spirit or devil that had taken up root inside the body was as old as the Bible and beyond, and the signs and symptoms of possession were well documented by the time of the Warboys case.[50] In *Guide to Grand-jury Men*, Bernard lists as being amongst the most common symptoms: extraordinary strength, raving, being deprived of sight, hearing or speech, speaking in a strange fashion, and speaking of things that they could not know through usual means. Being abused bodily and being seen to be greatly tormented by fits was also standard in such cases.[51] Violent reactions to mentions of God or the observance of religious acts such as prayer were also signs of the possessed, all of which symptoms mirrored those experienced by the Throckmorton daughters during their periods of 'illness'.

The link between witchcraft and possession was also firmly forged during the sixteenth century, a development of the traditional possession narrative that reflected the belief that witches were capable of, and often resorted to, sending spirits to torment their victims. With the Throckmorton children displaying all the classic signs of possession therefore, it was not a huge leap at all to decide that it was a witch who was responsible for their condition. The targeting of children or those less able to defend themselves, spiritually or physically, in place of the intended target was another common theme within the witch/possession relationship.[52] In light of this, it would have made perfect sense to anyone reading the story that Alice and her family had sent their spirits after the innocent girls when they found themselves powerless to harm the devout souls of their parents.[53]

Then of course there is the possibility that only Alice and John Samuel dared to voice: the girls were outright frauds, their suffering and fits nothing but malicious fakery. Indeed, there are several points during the story where it appears that Alice especially is being directly punished for daring to suggest that there might be anything other than truth in what the girls were saying, the 'victims' acting with a dogged determination to bring the old woman to not only confess, but also to accept and admit their version of reality.[54] This theory brings with it the question of whether the girls would be able to so consistently maintain their charade for such a long period of time, and how, if so, they managed to keep their stories straight amongst themselves and before others.

It was said that Alice and her friend Cicely Burder were known to be witches; it is possible that there had been talk about the women in the village before the onset of Jane's illness, and that the girls, consciously or subconsciously, used what they had heard to concoct their devastating story.[55] As far as their apparently 'clairvoyant' pronouncements were concerned, these can be explained; the manor house was actually not very large, and with there being a choice of only four rooms where Alice could be (three, if the one that the girls were in was removed from the equation), then the ability for the spirits to judge where she was at any given time begins to appear a little less remarkable.[56] This does leave the question of why they would do such a thing, as there is precious little evidence of motive against Alice other than her 'unclean' living. They may not have set out with a plan to bring the family down, and it might have started as something of a bit of fun, the whole matter getting fatally out of hand and leaving the girls unable to back down. The fact that the fits increased when there were more witnesses about could be seen as evidence that they were faking, and although the concept of them being driven to suicide is shocking, it is worth noting that – as in other similar cases – these attempts conveniently only took place when there was a certainty that they would be stopped and prevented from causing actual harm to themselves. It has also been suggested by several commentators that the fits served a two-fold purpose for the girls; both to avoid paying attention or complying with demands when they didn't want to do something, or, the flip side, to get the attention they desired when and how they desired it.[57]

Whether the girls themselves believed what they were saying and that their sufferings were real is a very interesting point and one that, regrettably, can only be speculated on. Perhaps the feverish Jane did indeed take fright at the sight of Alice Samuel that fateful November day; only for her tortured imaginings to spiral out of control in a most deadly fashion. It is possible that what took place in the Throckmorton household was not entirely voluntary; however it might have started out, there is an argument for a form of hysteria, that then spread through the girls and on to household staff alike.[58]

As in many cases, it is likely that a combination of factors came together to create the fatal situation in Warboys, made all the more tragic as, 'had either the will to believe amongst the adults or the capacity to persuade amongst the children faltered even for a while, the supernatural fog through which everything was being viewed would quickly have evaporated.'[59]

Another interesting point that comes out of the account is that regarding the legalities of the practice of scratching a witch to both prove her guilt and remove her power over a victim. Although a frequent occurrence in accounts of witchcraft accusations, the Warboys pamphlet makes several mentions of how the Throckmortons would not see Alice scratched because they knew it to be illegal.[60] Gilbert Pickering too, however fervent he might be in his desire to rout-out a witch, did not hold with the practice, upholding the theological advice both he and the Throckmortons had received against it. The reason for this was that it placed the scratcher in a somewhat dubious position – by carrying out the act, they were taking on the role of the witch and placing the witch in the role of victim, something that muddied the waters considerably.[61]

The idea behind scratching a witch was simple; it acted to break the power of the witch over the victim. It also acted as a method of proving witchcraft, as in the example of one of the Throckmorton girls refusing to scratch any hand but that of Alice's, despite being in a fit and having her face turned away, and thus, in theory, unable to tell who owned the hands set beside her.[62] The word 'scratch' is perhaps misleading; the brutality with which such attacks occurred in many cases constituted grievous assault against the suspect.

The diversion in the account regarding the involvement of Lady Cromwell and her fate is an intriguing one. The charge that the Samuels were responsible for causing her death by witchcraft made up the first of the three indictments against the accused, and it was, under the 1563 Witchcraft Act, the only one that would have meant death for the Samuels if and when they were found guilty.[63] Her death is also the only one ascribed to Alice Samuel and her family, and it is possible that it was included by the more legally savvy Throckmortons and their supporters in order to facilitate the complete removal of the Samuels from the picture.

Although Alice initially denied any knowledge or involvement in the death, on Sunday 25 March a conversation between Joan Throckmorton and the spirit Smack revealed further 'details' of the sorry story. Alice had indeed bewitched Lady Cromwell but then had regretted her actions; it was too late, and she was unable to perform the necessary unwitching to release her victim. At her failure, Alice turned to her husband for help, but neither John Samuel nor their daughter Agnes were able to undo the spell cast by Alice. There was a simple solution according to her daughter: if she could not cure Lady Cromwell, Agnes told her mother, she should kill her. Whatever illness really caused the death of the lady, Alice confessed to the murder on the gallows, by that point having seemingly been brought to fully believe in the crimes laid at her door.[64]

It is interesting to note that, after the execution of the Samuels, the Throckmorton family do not seem to have tarried long in Warboys.[65] Perhaps there was more fallout to the case than the account leads the reader to believe, or perhaps they belatedly felt some remorse at sending the family to their deaths.[66] What happened to the girls themselves who had set the deadly chain of events in motion? It would be incredibly fascinating to know how they reacted individually to their parts in the deaths of the Samuels family, but, as so often where thoughts and emotions from the past are involved, we can only speculate. Whether they felt remorse or guilt, or suffered future psychological effects, or whether they instead shrugged off this period of their lives never to revisit it cannot be known. What we can uncover is that the Throckmorton sisters married into local gentry families, their prospects unharmed by what had occurred in their childhood.[67]

It can be argued that no one truly benefited from what happened. The Samuels were wiped out, their other potential relations leaving the village, and the Throckmortons likewise found it necessary to move on. Even Henry Cromwell, the local lord and therefore recipient of the goods and money remaining to John Samuel and his family, did not keep it; the money was used to fund sermons each year on the terrible crime of witchcraft.

The Warboys case continued to intrigue and perplex readers greatly over the centuries that followed, and the story of the suffering girls proved to be hugely influential in a number of ways. The famous demoniac William Perry is known to have read the pamphlet describing the case and therefore can be cited as an influence on his own – faked – possession symptoms.

The notorious Anne Gunter likewise admitted to both reading it and to the influence it had upon her.[68] In a sense, the detailed pamphlet acted as a 'How To' guide for faking possession, outlining the behaviours that would convince an audience of the authenticity of a 'victim's' claims. It is also believed that the case was instrumental in the formulation of the 1604 Witchcraft Act, placing the case – and the Samuel family – at the heart of the historical narrative of England's witch trials.

Chapter 3

Families at War:
The Pendle Witches – 1612

Upon the arraignment and trial of these Witches at the last
Assizes and General Gaol delivery holden at Lancaster, we
found such apparent matters against them, that we thought
it necessary to publish them to the world.

The Wonderful Discoverie – Thomas Potts

Pendle Forest and nearby Pendle Hill are, even today, mired in myth and legend.
Lying a few miles outside of Lancaster, the forest was not the woodland that
the name implies; instead it was, and remains, an area of moorland known for
its rich hunting prospects.[1] On this land families lived and worked, livestock
was tended, and its inhabitants did business with those who lived in the
surrounding towns and villages.

Amongst those who lived there at the start of the seventeenth century were
the families of Southern and Whittle. Often impoverished, they eked out a
living through begging, occasional work when they could get it, and, it was
said, driving fear into the hearts of those who lived nearby. For the members
of these families were known locally to be witches, with the power to not
only help and heal, but also to punish and harm whoever they chose.

    The heads of these two families were Elizabeth Southern, known as
Old Demdike – coming from the ominous meaning of 'Devil Woman' –
and Anne Whittle, better known as Old Chattox.[2] Although initially good
friends, in 1601 Old Chattox and Old Demdike quarrelled. The cause of this
was a break-in at the house of Elizabeth Device, Old Demdike's daughter.
Elizabeth and her daughter Alizon found the majority of their linen missing,
along with some meal, their losses totalling close to twenty shillings, an
amount they could ill afford. To further add insult to injury, when out walking

the following Sunday, the two women spotted some of their missing goods in the possession of none other than one of Old Chattox's daughters. Certain they had caught the thief, Elizabeth and Alizon confronted the woman, and in a heated exchange a headband and cap were taken back as the Devices reclaimed what was theirs.

With the two families now decidedly at odds and despite the protection of his mother-in-law's reputation for witchcraft, Elizabeth's husband John Device was concerned enough to make a deal with Old Chattox. He would pay a measure of meal to her as a yearly tribute, in return for a promise not to use her powers to harm him or his family. This annual tribute was paid regularly until around eleven years later when, after a missed payment, John Device fell ill and died. On his deathbed he voiced his belief that this was no natural death: Chattox was to blame, having bewitched him in payback for his tardiness. The stresses and strains between the two families that had rumbled along just below the surface were thus reignited, though it is unlikely that anyone involved could have predicted the terrible outcome of events to follow.

Now a young woman of around 18, Alizon Device, whilst out begging one day, met a pedlar named John Law. She asked the man for some pins, and although accounts of what actually transpired between the two are conflicting, as they parted the pedlar stumbled. Unbeknownst to Alizon, by the time he managed to reach a nearby inn, John Law was completely lame down one side of his body, a condition he was quick to attribute to punishment from the young woman for not giving her the pins she requested. Summoned to his father's bedside, Abraham Law was quick to act, bringing complaints against Alizon to Roger Nowell, local Justice of the Peace.

Nowell, spurred by this tale and a history of similar local complaints surrounding the Devices, decided to fully investigate the mutterings about the families of the Forest of Pendle. Subsequently, on 30 March 1612, Alison Device, along with her mother Elizabeth and her brother James, were called in to be questioned.

During her examination, Alizon spoke out against her grandmother, the almost-blind Old Demdike. She related how she often accompanied the old woman as they went begging in the local area, before the story took a more fantastical turn: two years previously, Demdike had tried to persuade Alizon to let a 'Devil or familiar' come to her. If she did, her grandmother promised, she could ask it to do whatever she wanted. All she had to do in return was let it suck a little at her body.

Alizon had also witnessed her grandmother practising witchcraft herself. When a cow belonging to John Nutter, a farmer from near Newchurch, fell sick, he asked Demdike to come and offer her assistance in curing the animal. Agreeing, Demdike had asked Alizon to lead her outside. Despite it being about ten at night, the old woman had remained outside for about half an hour, before asking Alizon to again lead her back into the house. Although she did not witness exactly what went on, Alizon voiced her suspicions to Nowell that whatever took place did not bode well for the cow: they heard the next day that the animal was dead, with Alizon of the opinion that her grandmother had bewitched it to an unnatural end.

As she talked, Alizon provided more details of local tensions involving Old Demdike. Farmer Richard Baldwin had quarrelled with her grandmother two years previously and as a result he wouldn't allow her onto his land. A few days after the falling-out, Demdike had asked Alizon to take her outside, again at about ten o'clock at night; the old woman had stayed outside for about an hour. Again, Alizon swore she had no idea what her grandmother did during that time, but she feared it had not been good; the next morning she had learned that Baldwin's daughter had fallen ill, and the child had remained unwell for the space of a year before finally dying. Alizon had heard her grandmother cursing Baldwin several times after their argument, and she believed therefore that Demdike had bewitched the child to death in revenge.

Furthermore, something strange had happened to a pail of milk that Alizon had managed to beg. Leaving it in the house with her grandmother for half an hour whilst she went out, she had returned to discover butter waiting for her. Not so remarkable in itself, but not only had there been no sign of any butter when she went out, there was also the same amount of milk remaining in the pail. Old Demdike had not, Alizon was also certain, left the house during her absence.

Along with confessing her own crimes and relationship with the Devil, Alizon implicated Chattox and her family. She told Nowell about the incident with the break-in at the Device home, and how they had seen the stolen goods being worn by Chattox's daughter soon after. More damningly, she related how her father had been so certain of Chattox's ability to do the family harm through witchcraft that he had made the deal to pay a yearly tribute to the old woman in return for their safety, immunity which was swiftly revoked upon non-payment and the cause, Alizon swore, of her father's death. She had seen further first-hand evidence of Chattox's power and vengeful nature; two years previously she, Alizon, had been at the Nutter household, as she was friends with Anthony Nutter's daughter, Anne. The two girls had been laughing and chatting together, but Chattox had taken offence, declaring that the girls were laughing at *her*. Greatly displeased at this perceived lack of respect, Chattox had told them she would 'meet' with one of them, implying she would get her own back. Sure enough, Anne Nutter had fallen ill the day after and was dead three weeks later. It was not just Alizon saying such things either; rumours about Chattox abounded in the local area. She had heard say that Chattox was suspected of bewitching drink belonging to John Moore, a gentleman of Higham, and that she, Alizon, had herself heard Chattox vowing to have vengeance on the man. Sure enough, one of Moore's children fell sick, as Anne Nutter had, and after suffering for six months, this child too died. To further prove the old woman's part in the matter, Alizon had seen her sitting with a picture made of clay in her apron – something she tried to conceal from Alizon. When she mentioned this to her mother Elizabeth, her mother had been of the opinion that it was in the form of Moore's child. There was reason for the dislike of the Moore family; six or seven years earlier, Chattox had fallen out with Henry Moore after the man accused Chattox of bewitching some of his cattle. Chattox had talked against Moore in response and cursed him, speaking of revenge; he had been taken ill and died six months later, but not before holding Chattox responsible on his deathbed.

Alizon's brother James Device likewise incriminated their grandmother. A month earlier he had been on his way to his mother's house when he had seen a brown dog coming towards him from the direction of Demdike's. A couple of nights later at the same place – ten roods away from his grandmother's house – he had heard a terrible sound: that of many children shrieking and crying most horribly.[3] Both of these events had occurred in the evening.[4] Less than a week after this unsettling experience, James had been about twenty roods from the house just after dawn when he had heard more noise, this time like a group of cats yelling and shrieking, though there were no such animals to be seen. If he were not already convinced that there was something strange going on regarding his grandmother's house, three nights later he experienced something strange and frightening whilst in bed. Around midnight, something black about the size of a cat or hare came into his bedroom; it lay on him for about an hour, 'very heavily'.[5]

As James talked, he also implicated his sister. About 29 June the previous year, Henry Bullock had visited Demdike to complain that Alizon had bewitched his child and to request that the girl go with him to his house to see the result of what she had done. According to James, Alizon did so and, as she had told him later, 'fell down on her knees, and asked the said Bullock forgiveness, and confessed to him, that she had bewitched the said child.'[6]

With the family already firmly implicated in witchcraft by the two young people, on 30 March, Elizabeth Device also found herself before Nowell. She told the justice that her mother, Demdike, had a 'place on her left side by the space of forty years', where she suckled her familiars, and she had been a witch for that many years.[7] Things were not looking very good for the matriarch of the Device family at all.

That same day, Abraham Law, the son of the pedlar who had allegedly fallen foul of Alizon Device, also gave evidence. He related how on 21 March he had received an urgent letter summoning him to see his father, John Law, who lay sick in Colne. When he arrived, Abraham found his father in a most pitiful state, unable to speak and, apart from his eye, entirely lame down his left side. Shortly after his arrival his father recovered the ability to speak a little again, and he had complained that he felt as if his body was being sharply pricked with 'knives, elsons and sickles.'[8] This was, his father had gone on to tell him, exactly the same sensation as when he had encountered Alizon Device. The young woman had asked to buy some pins from him and when he discovered that she had no money, he had given her some anyway, for all the good it did him; Alizon had bewitched him and this illness was the result.[9] Alizon had not been satisfied with that however; far from leaving him alone, she had continued to come to him in the time that followed, lying on him and causing him great discomfort. The pedlar also talked against another woman, this one much older, who was involved in the business, but, said Abraham Law, his father did not know her name.[10]

In an attempt to alleviate his father's suffering, Abraham Law had gone in search of the young woman who was undoubtedly responsible for his torment; his search was successful, and he had found Alizon and taken her to his father only the day before. With witnesses present, John Law had accused Alizon of bewitching him; Alizon had not denied it, instead begging forgiveness on her knees, which his father had duly given.

As a result of this questioning and the answers given, on 2 April Alizon's grandmother Demdike, Old Chattox and her daughter Anne Redferne, were likewise summoned before Nowell.

Far from denying what was put to her, Demdike explained to the justice how she had become a witch. Twenty years before, she had been on her way home after begging, when, near a stonepit in Goldshaw, she met a spirit. In the shape of a boy, he wore a coat that was half black and half brown, and he had told her that if she gave him her soul, anything she wanted would be hers for the taking. When Demdike had asked the boy his name, he had replied that it was Tibb. The idea of having whatever she wanted when she had so little and was reduced to begging was too tempting to resist, and Demdike therefore consented to give away her soul in return for earthly satisfaction. Over the next five or six years, Tibb came to her many times, usually around evening, asking what she would have him do for her. Despite being in need, she had always told him that there was nothing she wanted him to do for her at that point. As the sixth year passed, things changed; one Sunday morning Demdike had been dozing with her child on her knee when Tibb appeared as a brown dog, asking to suck blood from her. She allowed him to do so, and he had taken the offering from under Demdike's arm. Perhaps horrified at what she had done, Demdike strove to send the spirit away, the words 'Jesus save my child', sending him from the room. She had indeed saved her child, but not herself; Demdike had, by her own admission, been left raving mad for the space of eight weeks afterwards.[11] The spirit had evidently returned after that point, and Demdike had been practising witchcraft ever since.

By her own account, even partially blind as she was, the elderly Demdike was clearly a force to be reckoned with; when Elizabeth Device was not paid for work she had carried out for Richard Baldwin at his mill, she asked her mother to accompany her to demand that she be compensated. The meeting did not go as planned; Baldwin, telling the two women to 'get out of my ground whores and witches, I will burn the one of you and hang the other'.[12] Rashly, and by her own admission, Demdike had responded, 'I care not for thee, hang thy self.'[13] As they rounded the next field, Tibbs, her spirit familiar, had appeared and, like all the best tempters appearing at moments of weakness, told her to get her revenge on the man. Demdike had needed no further persuading; she told Tibbs to exact revenge on her behalf, either on Baldwin himself or on his family, and the spirit vanished. This was, she said, the last time she had seen Tibb and did not know what had become of him.

Chattox was also questioned the same day, this former friend and, some said, pupil of Demdike's giving a somewhat different spin to what had been said against her. There had been an occasion when she had been asked by John Moore's wife to come and help with drink that was bewitched. She had gone, and said a charm that she was confident would put things right again only for Moore's wife to act in a most ungrateful manner; instead of being thankful, the woman had been aggrieved that she had used such a charm in her presence.[14] This was the reason she had called on her own spirit, 'Fancy', to go and do ill to one of Moore's cows by biting it on the head to make it go mad. The spirit did so in the form of a brown dog, and the cow was dead six weeks later.

Chattox also admitted to sending Fancy to kill a cow belonging to Anthony Nutter. Jealousy played a part in this act, as she suspected the man of preferring Demdike to herself, a slight that she took much to heart and was determined to avenge.

There was a price to pay for her actions; although giving her the power to perform such acts, Fancy had also been the cause of her being now almost completely blind. Furthermore, this particular relationship between witch and familiar was somewhat tempestuous; Fancy had appeared to her several times in the threatening form of a bear and on their last meeting – over a year earlier – he had pulled her down roughly when she had refused to speak with him.

The result of this round of questioning was that Chattox, her daughter Anne Redferne, Demdike and Alizon Device were imprisoned at Lancaster Castle to await trial at the next assizes. Elizabeth and James Device were left at liberty for the time being, as Nowell perhaps felt he had the most dangerous elements safely under lock and key.

It would appear that he was wrong; the imprisonment of the women was only the beginning of a series of events that would no doubt leave the justice wishing he had been more strident. Within a week of the arrests, it seems that those who remained at liberty were far from idle; in the version of events that finally reached Nowell's ears, the remaining Devices and their friends began plotting. On 10 April, a meeting of local 'witches' took place at Malkin Tower, Demdike's home, consisting of 'all the most dangerous, wicked, and damnable witches in the county far and near'.[15] It was something of a grand affair as these things went, with James Device stealing and killing a 'wether' (a castrated sheep) from John Robinson to feed the several people who gathered there. The purpose of the meeting was manifold: firstly, it was said to have been to discuss the naming of the familiar spirit belonging to the absent Alizon Device (suggesting that the meeting had been first planned before her imprisonment). Secondly, and more pressingly, talk turned to how to free those who were imprisoned, many of whom were related to those in attendance. After much deliberation, it was eventually decided that Thomas Covell, the jailer of the castle, was to be killed and, most spectacularly, the castle itself was to be blown up as part of this bold escape attempt.[16]

One of those who attended the gathering was Jennet Preston from Gisburn. She had come to seek help for the murder of Thomas Lister, revenge for his attempting to have her imprisoned at the previous York Assizes. She was not powerful enough to kill him by her own magic, so she asked the gathered witches for help, something to which they apparently agreed.

The meeting appears to have been considered successful, the women and three men in attendance departing on horseback after agreeing they would meet in a year's time at the house of Jennet Preston, where she promised them a great feast.

That was never to be. News of the meeting reached the ears of Justice Nowell, and as a result further enquiries were held. In the aftermath, several more arrests were made, with Elizabeth Device, her son James, Alice Nutter, Jane Bulcock and her son John, Isabel Roby, Margaret Pearson and Katherine Hewit committed to the castle from which they had hoped to liberate their friends and family.[17] With this new development, and victory well within his grasp, Nowell spared nothing in gathering as much evidence and information as he could against the suspected witches he held.

On 27 April, James Device was questioned again. Although some of what he said appears to be missing in the account of the case, what we do have is colourful indeed. James told Nowell how twelve years earlier Chattox had helped herself to three skulls from a churchyard, and upon removing eight teeth in total she had kept four and given the other four to his grandmother Demdike. The four teeth were actually produced, having been found by James Device and Henry Hargrieves, buried at the west end of Demdike's house. A clay picture had also been discovered close by; almost completely decomposed and unrecognisable, James insisted it was that of Anne Nutter, Anthony Nutter's deceased daughter.

Elizabeth Device, James and Elizabeth's mother, was also questioned. Initially she refused to admit anything, but Nowell had an ace up his sleeve; Jennet Device, Elizabeth's younger daughter, had been prevailed upon to reveal information about her family and, most damningly, the meeting at Malkin Tower. When she discovered this, and also that James and Alizon had spoken against her, Elizabeth caved, as Nowell had no doubt expected her to.

She confessed that she also had a spirit named Ball; it had come to her as a brown dog whilst she was in her mother's house. Four years earlier the spirit had told her to make a picture of clay in the likeness of John Robinson; she had done so and dried it out over the space of a week – a week after the picture was completely crumbled, the man himself had died. When asked why she had taken against Robinson, Elizabeth admitted it was because he had taken her to task for having a 'bastard child' with a man named Seller.

As more people talked, it became clear that Old Demdike was believed to be the driving force behind the local network of witches in the Pendle area. For a start, she had involved the rest of her family in her wicked ways: her son Christopher Howgate, daughter Elizabeth Device, and her grandchildren James and Alizon were all variously implicated. She was the very worst of all the witches, and, after being a witch for fifty of her eighty years, the root of all the trouble that had taken place. She was also responsible for the initiation of her then friend Anne Whittle, alias Chattox, into a life of witchcraft.

In a way that would no doubt displease those with a keen eye for justice, Old Demdike herself did not live to see trial, dying in prison before she could face judgement in court. Chattox and her daughter Anne Redferne, Elizabeth, Alizon and James Device, Alice Nutter, Katherine Hewit, John and Jane Bulcock, Isabel Roby and Margaret Pearson had no such escape and came before judges and jury on 18 and 19 August 1612, accused in total of the deaths of over a dozen people between them.[18]

At the bar, Chattox was arraigned for the murder of Robert Nutter, to which she pleaded not guilty. After relating how she had come to have her spirit, Fancy, she explained why she had cause to dislike Robert Nutter: her daughter, Anne Redferne, was a tenant of the Nutter family, and eighteen or so years previously the young man had made unwanted advances towards her. When rebuffed, Nutter had responded angrily, threatening that she would never stay on the land if he inherited. Having resisted using Fancy to do any harm prior to this, Chattox had, in her anger, called the spirit to her. Chattox instructed him that she wanted him to go and get revenge for her upon Robert Nutter. The young man had died about three months later. There were others who were as guilty of his death as she: Elizabeth Nutter (the wife of old Robert Nutter), Jane Boothman and 'Loomeshaws wife of Burley' had also come to her to ask for Robert Nutter's death, saying that if he was gone they would be free to inherit the land themselves. She had refused to do so for them at the behest of her son-in-law, Thomas Redferne; Chattox was of the opinion that the other women had taken matters into their own hands and were as responsible for the death of Robert Nutter as she herself might be.

Elizabeth Device's family connections went against her as she too stood before the judges, as,

> it is very certain, that amongst all these witches there was not a more dangerous and devilish witch to execute, having old Demdike, her mother, to assist her; James Device and Alizon Device, her own natural children, all provided with spirits, upon any occasion of offence ready to assist her.[19]

There were several indictments against her; the bewitching to death of John Robinson, doing the same to James Robinson, and, along with the deceased Demdike and Alice Nutter, causing the death by witchcraft of Henry Mitton. On all three counts Elizabeth pleaded not guilty, despite having confessed previously to having committed these acts.

Once again, it was the production of her daughter, the 9-year-old Jennet, that proved Elizabeth's downfall.[20] However calm she may have been beforehand, at the sight of the child Elizabeth Device broke down, shouting and raving at Jennet, making all manner of threats in a desperate attempt to keep her from talking. Finally Elizabeth was removed from the courtroom, allowing Jennet the space to repeat her previous words against her family and their friends. Her mother was a witch, and she had seen her familiar spirit on several occasions, and knew that her mother had sent it to kill the two Robinson men and Henry Mitton. James Device's evidence was also produced regarding the discovery of the clay images and intent to bewitch John Robinson. Despite this, when asked what she had to say in response, Elizabeth, returned to the room after Jennet had finished, continued to insist upon her own innocence, shouting against those who had given evidence to the contrary.[21] Finally crushed, Elizabeth's only recourse now was to cry out for mercy to the court as she was finally led away.

James Device himself was the next to stand before the court, and the figure he presented must have greatly shocked those in attendance. James was 'so insensible, weak, and unable in all things, as he could neither speak, hear, or stand, but was holden up when he was brought to the place where of his arraignment to receive his trial.'[22] Despite his state he managed to indicate that he pleaded not guilty to the charges of bewitching Anne Townley and John Duckworth to death. His sister Jennet's evidence against him was produced, and it was clear that things would not go in his favour.

That day Chattox, Elizabeth Device and James Device were all found guilty of the indictments against them, only Anne Redferne escaping condemnation when she was found not guilty of the charge of murdering Robert Nutter through witchcraft.

The following day, 19 August, saw the remaining Pendle suspects before the court to face their fates. Despite being found innocent of the murder of Robert Nutter the day before, Anne Redferne was not so lucky this time around; she was found guilty of murdering Christopher Nutter by the same means. John and Abraham Law were presented to give evidence against Alizon Device for her part in causing the former's suffering, and she was likewise found guilty.

The star of the show this day was again Jennet Device, and she was used to identify several of the 'witches' she stated were at the meeting at Malkin Tower. Presented with a group of women and asked to pick out those she recognised, the young girl did so, correctly identifying Alice Nutter, Katherine Hewit and others who had been there that night. Not only that, but Jennet was able to say with convincing confidence where they had sat and what had been spoken of, a damning indictment against those who pleaded their innocence. Although several of the accused pleaded not guilty, as on the previous day, confessions made earlier to Nowell were now read out against them, leaving the prisoners with little recourse as they had been condemned by their own words along with those of the witnesses produced against them. Repentance was shown by Chattox, as she cried and begged for forgiveness for her daughter, but most remained resolutely insistent on their innocence.[23]

The final outcome was that Elizabeth, Alizon and James Device, Chattox and her daughter, Alice Nutter, John and Jane Bulcock, Katherine Hewit and Isobel Roby, were all found guilty and condemned to death with the words:

> You shall all go from hence to the Castle, from whence you came; from thence you shall be carried to the place of Execution for this County: where your bodies shall bee hanged until you are dead; and God have mercy upon your souls.[24]

¶A true and iuſt Recorde, of
the Information, Examination
and Confeſsion of all the Witches, taken at
S. Oſes in the countie of Eſſex: whereof
ſome were executed, and other ſome entreated according to the determination of lawe.

Wherein all men may ſee what a peſtilent
people Witches are, and how vnworthy to lyue
in a Chriſtian Common-
wealth.

Written orderly, as the ca-
ſes were tryed by euidence,
By W. W.

¶Imprinted in London at the
three Cranes in the Vinetree by
Thomas Dawſon
1582.

Title page of *A True and Just Record*, the main contemporary source for the accusations against Ursula Kemp.

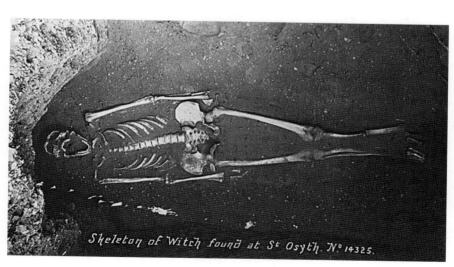

Skeleton of Witch found at St Osyth. No. 14325.

The skeleton of 'Ursula' from 1921.

'Ursula' undergoing examination to ascertain the identity of the skeleton.

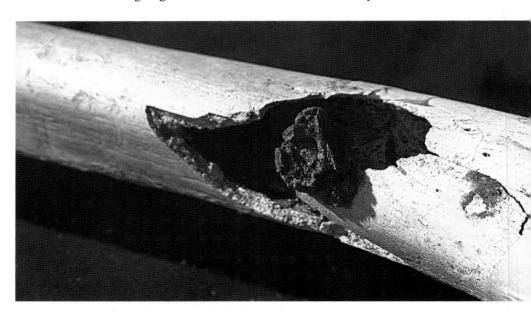
Bone from 'Ursula' with nail fragment visible.

A woodcut showing witches gathering for a meal with Devils.

Warboys Manor House where the Throckmorton children made their deadly accusations against Alice Samuel.

Warboys Manor House from the east side.

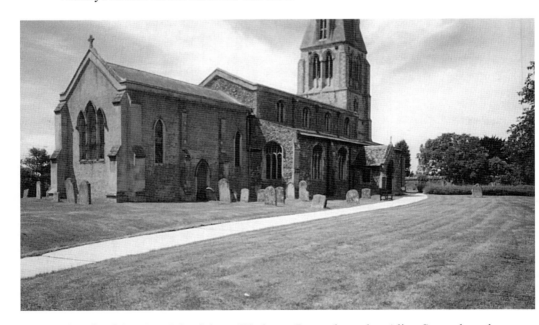

Church of St Mary Magdalene, Warboys. It was here that Alice Samuel made her confession in front of the gathered congregation before retracting it the following day.

Interior of Huntingdon gaol.

View of the gaol from the outside.

The location of the gallows, where the Samuel family met their end, as it looks today.

Read Hall, where Roger Nowell interrogated Alizon Device.

Lancaster Castle.

The Trough of Bowland – The 'Pendle Witches' took this route on their way to trial in 1612.

A ruined barn at Bull Hole Farm, home to the Nutter family who spoke out against Anne Redferne and others.

GRAVE ON SOUTH SIDE OF ST. MARY'S CHURCH, NEWCHURCH-IN-PENDLE

A grave said to be that of Alice Nutter, in the graveyard of St Mary's Church, Newchurch-in-Pendle.

MATTHEW HOPKINS,
OF MANNINGTREE, ESSEX,
THE CELEBRATED WITCH-FINDER.

Matthew Hopkins, the infamous 'Witchfinder General'.

HOPKINS.THE WITCH FINDER.

A late eighteenth-century depiction of Matthew Hopkins.

Many of the familiars reported by Hopkins and Stearne had suspiciously outlandish names.

Depiction of a 'witch swimming', as experienced by John Lowes and many others under the direction of Hopkins and Stearne.

Francis Hutchinson was greatly
intrigued by Lowes's story.

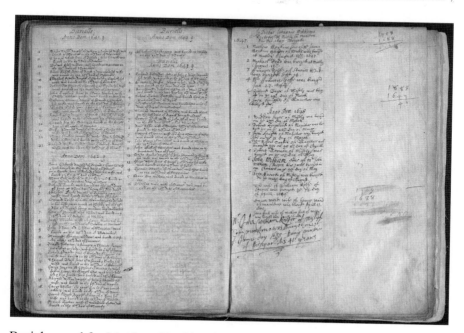

AN
Hiſtorical ESSAY
CONCERNING
WITCHCRAFT.
WITH
OBSERVATIONS upon MATTERS OF
FACT ; tending to clear the Texts of the
Sacred Scriptures, and confute the vulgar
Errors about that Point.

AND ALSO

TWO SERMONS: One in Proof of the
Chriſtian Religion ; The other concerning the
Good and Evil Angels.

By FRANCIS HUTCHINSON, D. D.
Chaplain in Ordinary to His Majeſty, and Mini-
ſter of St. *James*'s Pariſh in St. *Edmund's-Bury*.

PSALM XXXI. 6.
*I have hated them that hold ſuperſtitious Vanities : but
I truſt in the Lord.*

1 TIM. IV. 7.
*But refuſe profane and old Wives Fables, and exerciſe
thy ſelf rather unto Godlineſs.*

LONDON:
Printed for R. KNAPLOCK, at the *Biſhop's Head*, and
D. MIDWINTER, at the *Three Crowns* in St. *Paul's*
Church-yard. MDCCXVIII.

Burial record for Matthew Hopkins from the Parish Church of Mistley.

Entry from John Andrew's Trust Account Book showing aid given to Temperance Lloyd and Widow Edwards in 1679.

Further entries from the John Andrews Trust Account Book for 1680-81, for Temperance Lloyd, Mary Trembles and Widow Edwards.

May 7th 1682° A greate disturbance in the parish Church
of Bideford betwene mr ogilby and mr ___ filed
Samuell Jones, Christopher Prust and ___
Bennett Dunscombe

15th June The oath of Allegiance generally taken by
all the Inhabitants of this towne ___
before mr fist mayo. and mr Davie Justice, ___ filed
in pursuant of an order made att the ___
Generall Sessions of the peace for the ___
County of Devon for the putting in ___
Execucon generall Lawes for the security ___
of the Kings Sacred person, and our Establishes
Religion and Government

5th July Severall Informacons against, together with
the Confession of Temperance Lloyd, for ___
practising of witchcraft, upon the body of, filed
Grace Thomas ___ The fifth sent by a
mittimus unto Goale, ___ found guilty att the
Assizes holden 14th August. ___ And Executed ___
the 25th the papers

18th July Mary Trembles and Susanna Edwards theire
Confession; together with severall Informacons
ag' them for practising of witchcraft upon filed
the bodyes of Grace Barnes the wife of John
Bideford aforesaid yeoman, and Dorcas
Coleman the wife of John Coleman of Bideford
aforesaid Marryner, ___ 19th sent by a
mittimus unto Goale ___ found guilty and ___
Executed as next above, the papers ___
Searches of theire bodyes upon oath theire filed
returne

21th July mr mayo. Lett to mr Hill the Towne Clerke
touching Mary Beare, and Elizabeth Caddy
with Severall Informacons ag' them filed
An' Mary Beare there was a presentmen,
But against Elizabeth Caddy (who was
out upon Baile) there was an Endictme
p'ferred by Mary Weekes, the wife of Rob'
Weekes of Bideford aforesaid sent. And
by the Grand Jury, returned with an ___
Ignoramus

26th July Severall Informacons ag' the said Susanna
Edwards for practising of witchcraft filed
upon the body of Dorcas Coleman the
wife of the said John Coleman of ___
Bideford Marryner ___

Memorand the said Susanna Edwards & Mary Trembles having Severally confessed
upon theire Examinacons That they said bewitched the said Grace Barnes
they could not be Endicted for the same Bitnes Sewally whereupon the said
Mary Trembles, was Endicted onely for practising of witchcraft upon the
said Grace Barnes, And the said Susanna was severally Endicted for ___
practising of witchcraft upon the body of the said Dorcas Coleman

Bideford Quarter Sessions Records for the Bideford Witches.

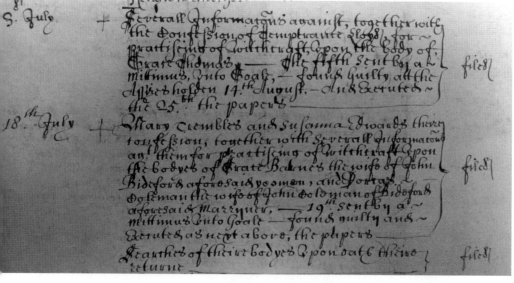

Enlarged section of the Quarter Sessions Records, showing information regarding Susannah Edwards bewitching Dorcas Coleman and Grace Barnes.

Enlarged section of the Quarter Sessions Records, recording the 'confessions' of the Bideford Witches.

Cottage believed to have been shared by the three witches from Bideford, long since burned down. There is, however, no evidence to support the tidy theory that the women lived together.

Plaque commemorating the Bideford Witches and Alice Molland.

Bideford Mural containing the controversial depiction of the 'Bideford Witches'. There are many who believe the image of the witches is disrespectful, sexist and damagingly stereotypical, while others maintain that it does the important task of keeping the memory of the injustice alive.

Margaret Pearson escaped the noose because although she was found guilty of witchcraft she had not caused the death of anyone, and therefore she was sentenced to four stints in the pillory throughout the year.

Jennet Preston had already met her fate; found guilty at York on 27 July, she was executed there on 29 July. Those who had been sentenced at Lancaster were hanged on 20 August 1612, and the Pendle Witches entered history as some of the most notorious witches in England.[25]

****

There are few witchcraft cases in England better known of than that of the Pendle Witches, and the fascination with the events and personalities involved remains strong to this day. The main source of evidence for the case, Thomas Potts's *The Wonderful Discovery of Witches in the County of Lancaster*, was printed within months of the events it records, a careful and detailed pamphlet that provides many intriguing glimpses into the world of the accused. It is perhaps the most well known and famous account of any witch trial in England, and also one of the most detailed, providing a rich source for historians and those with an interest in England's witch trials alike.

What is most striking about the Pendle case is the rich cast of characters presented to the reader. Demdike, Chattox and their respective families are brought to life, their personalities loud and bold on the page, and a picture of everyday life in the Pendle area is revealed. If the descriptions of the principal players are to be believed, then these notorious 'witches' fit perfectly with the popular image of how a witch should look and behave. Old Demdike was a 'damnable and malicious witch' who 'was a general agent for the Devil', being around 80 years of age and mostly blind. Chattox in turn was painted as 'a very old withered spent and decrepit creature, her sight almost gone', known for muttering and mumbling curses against others as she went about her business.[26] Elizabeth Device, recast in her mother's role after Demdike's death, was a 'barbarous and inhumane monster' of whom it was said that 'no man near her, neither his wife, children, goods, or cattle should be secure or free from danger.'[27] She was as terrible in appearance as she was in character as,

> this odious witch was branded with a preposterous mark in
> nature, even from her birth, which was her left eye, standing

lower than the other; the one looking down, the other looking up, so strangely deformed, as the best that were present ... did affirm they had not often seen the like.[28]

Whether these were accurate descriptions or not is lost to time, but such evocative imagery highlights how people expected, and therefore saw, the witches believed to be in their midst.

That rivalry of some nature existed between the families of Southern/ Device and Whittle is very much in evidence in the pamphlet account; the reader is told in no uncertain terms that if Old Demdike was for something or someone, then Chattox would be against it and vice versa. If reports were to be believed, this rivalry had fatal consequences, as it had been Anthony Nutter's perceived preference for Chattox's rival that induced her to send Fancy to kill his cow. Indeed, it is possible that it was this very competition that led to the undoing of both families, as the pair, 'having become keen rivals for the ... attendant emoluments derived from the dispensation of supposed devilish charms and more or less noxious potions, somewhat recklessly advertised their wares, vieing with each other in claiming responsibility for all the deaths and misfortunes of the countryside.'[29]

It is also clear that both families had a long-standing reputation for witchcraft and unpleasant behaviour, making them unpopular in the local area. As already mentioned, when Elizabeth Device had helped Richard Baldwin at his mill, she asked her mother, Old Demdike, to go there to request the payment she felt was her due. As they approached, Baldwin himself appeared and shouted at them, calling the two women whores and witches. This was not the only incident indicative of how people felt about the families. About six years before the events of the trial, Chattox's daughter Elizabeth had been begging at John Nutter's house where she was given milk; she took it to her mother in another field, where Chattox put it into a can and said a charm over it. John Nutter, happening by, expressed great displeasure with what the old woman was doing, kicking over the can in his annoyance, no doubt certain she was up to no good. What was more, eighteen or nineteen years before that, his brother, Christopher Nutter, had told his father Robert that he was certain he had been bewitched by Chattox and her daughter Anne Redferne. Despite his father's scepticism, Robert was adamant, to the point that he declared he would see them locked up himself upon his return from a visit to Wales with his master.[30]

Both the Southern and Whittle families were reputed to make use of magic to gain revenge upon those who displeased them. Alizon Device reported how Robert Baldwin had fallen out with her grandmother (probably in the wake of the incident regarding payment for Elizabeth Device's work) and as a consequence the old woman was not allowed onto his land. In retaliation, she believed Demdike had bewitched Baldwin's child to death. Anne Nutter died just weeks after Chattox believed the girl to be laughing at her. However petty, these slights were perceived by both the accused and the accuser to have been serious enough to warrant the drastic and deadly action that followed.[31]

One of the main methods believed to have been used by the women to gain revenge after verbal cursing was through the use of clay pictures or images. In its basic form, this involved creating a wax or clay figure to represent the intended victim. The image was then pricked or had pins stuck in the area where pain or illness was desired, with the victim then suffering accordingly. This was not an isolated belief; the idea of 'image magic' had been common since ancient times and was in consistent use from the Anglo Saxon period through to the reign of Elizabeth I and beyond.[32] A prevalent belief in the population as a whole, it is not therefore surprising to discover it within evidence given in the witch trials. Accordingly, Demdike was told by her spirit Tibbs that the quickest way to take a man's life was to make a figure of him in clay and then dry it. Once dry, it should be pricked to cause pain, and crumbled to cause wasting and eventual death.

Part of the evidence given by Demdike against Chattox was that half a year before Robert Nutter had died she, Demdike, went to the house of Thomas Redferne, Chattox's son-in-law. There she saw Chattox and her daughter, each on one side of the ditch with pictures of clay, and Chattox was busy making a third one whilst her daughter helped. As Demdike looked on, Tibb appeared to her as a cat, advising her to join the other women in their dubious activity. When Demdike asked what they were doing, Tibb told her that they were making three pictures: of Christopher Nutter, Robert Nutter and his wife Marie. It was the making of such images that had Anne Redferne branded as 'more dangerous than her mother, for she made all or most of the pictures of clay, that were made or found at any time'.[33]

Due to the nature of the trial, the focus of the account is understandably on the negative elements of the activities of the accused; even then, and despite their evident unpopularity, it is clear from the text that the women in question were also frequently called to help when their neighbours had exhausted more mundane methods of resolving a problem. Such examples include when Chattox was asked to un-witch the Moore family's drink (though she had received short shrift for her pains) and Demdike being called upon to heal the Nutters' cow. The two families clearly had a reputation for being able to perform both positive and negative magic, with those in the locality being willing to overlook the more dubious activities ascribed to the 'witches' when it suited their purpose. This illustrates an intriguing and common thread that is repeated throughout England's witch trials: the dual nature ascribed to those with a reputation for witchcraft, the ability to both harm and cure, and highlights that having such a reputation, for either good or ill, could be a dangerous thing indeed. Another prominent theme in the Pendle case is the familiar idea that witchcraft spread, almost like a disease, from friend to friend or from one generation of a family to another. Chattox had refused when the Devil first came to her and asked for her soul; it was her then friend Demdike who had slowly worn down her resistance until she agreed. Likewise, it was Demdike who had persuaded her granddaughter Alizon to allow a Devil to appear to her and to suck at her in return for getting what she wanted, and she had 'brought up her own children, instructed her grandchildren, and took great care and pains to bring them to be witches'.[34] She had clearly achieved her aim only too well, as Potts waxes lyrical in his account of the case, berating Elizabeth Device saying she was,

> beyond example; so far from sensible understanding of thy own misery, as to bring thy own natural children into mischief and bondage; and thy self to be a witness upon the gallows, to see thy own children, by thy devilish instructions hatched up in villany and witchcraft, to suffer with thee, even in the beginning of their time, a shameful and untimely death.[35]

The family element is further illustrated in the case of Jane Bulcock and her son John, the witchcraft of the one going far towards condemning the other.

Although not peculiar to this case, as has already been seen in both St Osyth and Warboys, the use of child testimony in the Pendle case stands out, not only for allowing evidence from those under the age of 14 in court (something which by the law of the time was illegal), but also the way in which it was used to bring down so many of the accused.

Between them, Jennet and James Device provided the bulk of the evidence against their accused families and friends.[36] It is unclear from the account just how old James Device was, but this 'youth' was almost certainly in his late teens or early twenties; generally presented as of unsound mind, and 'a youth of weak and childish intellect', the word of the 'unpredictable' young man was taken at face value to suit the case that was being made.[37] It is not clear whether James's instability was present before his arrest, (or to what extent the account of the trial exploited artistic license in describing him), and there has been some speculation as to whether James's condition was a direct result of his treatment during his imprisonment.[38]

The undoubted prize witness was young Jennet Device; 9 years old, 'pert, precocious and anxious to draw attention to herself', according to at least one commentator, it was the word of this girl – so short that she had to be stood on a table in the courtroom in order for her to be seen – that sealed the fate of those who stood trial.[39] According to Jennet, her brother James had been a witch for three years, starting when a black dog by the name of Dandy came to him and persuaded him into a life of witchcraft. Twelve months ago she had witnessed James calling for Dandy, asking for help in killing old Mistress Towneley in revenge for her having offended him. A week later, Jennet had been to the old woman's house and seen her in the kitchen; Mistress Towneley had looked decidedly ill, and it looked to Jennet as if James and Dandy were to blame. Furthermore, according to Jennet, James had caused the death of Blaze Hargrieves, sending Dandy once more to carry out the task.

Despite the girl's testimony being allowed in the courtroom as viable evidence, the judges were keen to at least appear to play by the rules. Jennet was apparently tested on several instances as to the truth of her words in an attempt to reveal any scope for lying. Accordingly, Jennet was removed from the room and the position of the prisoners rearranged; in addition to this, a person unconnected to the case was placed amongst them. Jennet was then brought back in and asked to identify the women that had been at Malkin Tower on that fateful Good Friday. Jennet passed the test with flying colours; she took Alice Nutter by the hand, not only saying that she had been there, but identifying where she had sat, who had been sat by her, and what they had talked about. Jennet repeated this process with Katherine Hewit, picking her out of the group with apparent ease. What further confirmed belief that Jennet told the truth was when

> My Lord Bromley being very suspicious of the accusation of
> Jennet Device, the little wench, commanded her to look upon

the prisoners that were present at Malkin Tower … she looked upon and took many by the hands, and accused them to be there, and when she had accused all that were present, she told his Lordship there was a woman that came out of Craven that was amongst the witches at the Feast, but she saw her not amongst the prisoners at the bar.[40]

This was none other than the absent Jennet Preston, who had already met her end on the gallows in York, confirming not only that a meeting had taken place, but also that the young girl knew exactly who had been present and who had not. To make completely certain, the judge questioned Jennet about a made up person, but Jennet was not to be tricked, stating firmly that she had never heard that name before nor knew a person called by it.[41]

It was clear that Jennet was something of a celebrity in the courtroom:

Which examinat, although she were but very young, yet it was wonderful to the court, in so great a presence and audience, with what modesty, government, and understanding, she delivered this evidence against the prisoner at the bar, being her own natural brother, which he himself could not deny, but there acknowledged in every particular to be just and true.[42]

It has to be wondered what was going through the girl's mind that day in court and when she had previously given evidence, and, more importantly, whether she understood in any way what her words would mean for her neighbours and family. Did Jennet understand that she was, effectively, sending them all to the gallows? If Jennet was unaware, her mother Elizabeth Device, was not; when she saw Jennet in the court room she,

according to her accustomed manner, outrageously cursing, cried out against the child in such fearful manner, as all the court did not a little wonder at her, and so amazed the child, as with weeping tears she cried out unto my Lord the Judge, and told him, she was not able to speak in the presence of her mother.[43]

One can only speculate as to whether she felt guilty or scared at that moment, or just plain bewildered amidst the noise and charged atmosphere of the court. There are many who are unwilling to give the girl the benefit of the doubt and it has been suggested that, on the contrary, Jennet knew exactly what she was doing, her actions being some sort of revenge against the family that had raised her. In this view, Jennet, the 'darling of the court' was far from a passive pawn, and 'The sweet child seems to have delighted in damning all her family.'[44] It has also been posited that Jennet was coached carefully for her starring role, either by Nowell or someone trusted by him with the task, so that the young girl knew exactly what she was to say and do.[45] Whatever the case, the girl played her part only too well, convincing not only the judge and jury but, if Potts's account is to be believed, also Jennet Preston's husband who was in attendance at the trial and left after Jennet gave her testimony convinced that his wife had deserved her death.[46]

There is an interesting follow-up where Jennet Device is concerned which has roused the curiosity of historians over the years following the tragic events at Lancaster because, in 1633, accusations of witchcraft came again to the area of Pendle. A 10-year-old boy, Edmund Robinson, related a fantastical tale of how he had witnessed a greyhound turn into local woman Frances Dickonson and another that turned into a young boy. Frances had then proceeded to turn the boy into a horse and taken Robinson with her on a ride to a gathering of fellow witches. There he saw several women he recognised, amongst them, one Jennet Device. Robinson made a bid for freedom and although the witches chased after him he was rescued, reporting what he had seen to his father and the local magistrates. As a result, several of the women he named as being present at the gathering were apprehended. Amongst them, 'Jennet' was searched and discovered to have 'two paps or marks in her secrets', and was accused of killing Isabel, wife of William Nutter.[47] There was considerable scepticism and interest regarding this new troop of Lancashire witches, and several were selected – Jennet was not amongst them – to visit the king himself in London. Although the case finally collapsed, largely due to the increasing scepticism of the time and Edmund Robinson himself finally admitting he had fabricated the stories, several of the accused women died in prison before they could be released, victims of the harsh privations of prison life. As for Jennet herself, her name was listed as one of the prisoners still imprisoned in Lancaster Castle in 1636, along with others who could not afford to pay for their release despite being cleared of the crime. Although the two Jennets being one and the same makes for a good story, there is another potential and more likely fate for Jennet. A burial entry from the church of St Mary's at Newchurch in Pendle reads: 'Jennet Sellar alias Devis'. With the burial taking place on 22 December 1635, this Jennet cannot have been the imprisoned witch who still languished under lock and key several months later.[48]

Amongst the many intriguing personalities involved in the Pendle case is the justice at the forefront of questioning the witches, Roger Nowell himself.[49] Well used to being in authority, Nowell had held the position of Sheriff two years previously and has been painted in several conflicting lights over the centuries that have followed the case. Some commentators have compared him unfavourably to the Justice behind the St Osyth trials, suggesting that, like Darcy, he was guilty of asking leading questions of suspects and witnesses and exploiting the weaknesses of those with less social and economic power than himself. Ewen refers to him as 'the zealous Nowell', convinced that the confessions of the Pendle witches were obtained through 'specious promises of favour'.[50] Barbara Rosen likewise echoes this view, referring to Nowell's 'tireless zeal' and making the link between him and Darcy.[51] Walter Bennett is another who does not hold the justice in high esteem, remarking that Nowell 'was most probably responsible for building up the whole affair of the Pendle Witches out of a few wild accusations made against old Demdike by a young girl who was herself a convicted thief'.[52]

Although it is tempting to paint all justices involved in such cases as rabid witch hunters with a hidden agenda, it is wise to tread cautiously before reaching that conclusion.[53] Given the belief structures of the day, it is viable to suggest that far from being merely 'a religious and gullible justice of the peace', after learning of events at Malkin Tower, Nowell and his fellow justices were firmly convinced they were facing a major outbreak of witchcraft that posed a serious threat to local order and the souls of those who lived under his jurisdiction.[54] It is equally possible that Nowell saw in the complaint made by Abraham Law against Alizon Device, a convenient excuse to remove several unpleasant characters who had been terrorising the local area for years.[55]

In reality, not a lot is actually known about Nowell's personal view on witches or his knowledge thereof. What is clear is that,

> Nowell was, certainly, vital in moving the 1612 witch prosecutions along, but it is unclear if he went in as a determined witch hunter, or if he was a gentleman with very much standard ideas of witchcraft who was sucked into an ever growing mass of accusations which became all the more convincing as witness after witness came to give evidence, and witch after witch confessed.[56]

There are various theories regarding Nowell's level of knowledge of witchcraft theory of the day, with some attributing to him a mere passing familiarity with James I's *Daemonologie,* whereas others state that he read extensively on the subject, knowing not only commentators such as William Perkins, but that he was also familiar with the Malleus Maleficarum and an avid reader of English witch-trial pamphlets.

One thing that *is* known for certain is that the justice had links to a previous witchcraft case through his family: Nowell was related through the first marriage of his mother to the Starkies of Huntroyd. Nowell's half-nephew, Nicholas Starkie, and his wife Anne experienced trouble in 1595: their two children, 12-year-old John and 10-year-old Anne, began to suffer from strange convulsions. Neither doctors – to the tune of £200 – nor a Catholic priest could do anything to help the children and so, in desperation, the parents turned to a wise man, Edmund Hartley, for help in curing the children, whom he was convinced were possessed by the Devil. Matters only got worse, culminating in the entire household erupting in hysteria, several others being bewitched, and Edmund Hartley himself ending his life at the gallows for causing the bewitchment in the household. Increasingly frantic, Starkie's next port of call was to ask famed astrologer John Dee for help, and it was on Dee's recommendation that Puritan ministers John Darrel and George More were invited to the Starkie house. The two men were apparently successful, freeing the possessed members of the household who then remained well.[57] By the time of events in Pendle, the Starkie and Nowell families were living close to each other, and it is highly likely that the events surrounding his half-nephew's family were not quick to be forgotten by Nowell.[58] It has therefore been put forward that both this background, and also his task of working with Thomas Lister regarding the second trial of Jennet Preston, set Nowell on his course as witch hunter in the trial of the Pendle Witches.[59]

Another figure at the forefront of the Pendle trial, and instrumental in deciding the fate of the accused, was Judge Sir Edward Bromley.[60] Having worked together for the previous two years, Nowell and Bromley were well acquainted, and it is likely that Nowell discussed the problems brewing in the Pendle area with Bromley and others both before and during the events that unfolded.[61] Like Nowell, Bromley has likewise come under fire, with Ewen commenting on his 'want of judicial ability' as highlighted by his remark to the innocent Samelsbury witches that they were as guilty as those who were condemned despite their being found technically innocent.[62] It has also been suggested that Bromley's remark serves as further evidence that some judges of the day were far from circumspect, with the desire to convict overriding the facts and a belief in justice.[63] Bromley has also been blasted for the fact that, 'The judges at the trial at Lancaster ... seem to have been biased against the prisoner for they did not point out the serious contradictions given in the evidences of witnesses.'[64] A further black mark rests against his name; before the 1612 trial at which he presided, there had never been a case of a judge condemning so many witches in one go, which might, one could be excused for thinking, suggest unwarranted overzealousness on Bromley's part, as well as a serious lack of judgement.[65]

The same words regarding the Salmesbury witches have also been counted in Bromley's favour, suggesting instead of a lack of judgement, rather a 'pragmatic sense of the legal system, highlighting again the need to tread carefully when making sweeping assumptions at such a far remove.'[66] Gibson highlights that Bromley was fully aware of the flaws of the legal system, as evidenced in his point of defending what took place in Lancaster.[67] It must also be noted that it was Bromley who presided over Jennet Preston's first Assize appearance in York during Lent 1612, at which she was found not guilty of the murder of a child belonging to the Dodgeson family. It has been posited therefore that the blame for the outcome at Lancaster should be laid instead at the door of Bromley's co-judge, Sir James Altham, whose influence on Bromley 'must be reckoned as a cause of the tragic outcome at Lancaster.'[68] It was, after all, Altham not Bromley who condemned Jennet Preston to death at her second trial, and this was not an outcome without precedent; Altham had likewise condemned a woman to death for witchcraft in Chelmsford in 1607. By contrast, this was the first time Bromley was known to have condemned someone accused of the crime.[69]

What cannot be forgotten is that 'One fact most manifest is that both judge and jury were firmly convinced of the existence of witchcraft.'[70] Indeed, Chattox and Demdike's reputations and power over their neighbours came only from people believing that they had the power they purported themselves to have. Those who spoke out against the accused clearly believed that they or their loved ones had been harmed by magic, and that those responsible were before them in the courtroom. Despite a general belief in the existence of magic and witchcraft however, there were some examples of scepticism in the Pendle story that should be highlighted. For example, John Nutter recalled how, when his brother Robert had told their father he believed Chattox or Anne Redferne had bewitched him, Christopher Nutter had dismissed the idea out of hand, declaring his son ridiculous.[71] This indicates that although there was a widespread belief in the ability to perform witchcraft this was far from a blind, automatic assumption; such beliefs or otherwise could be exercised with judgement and discretion. Alternatively, it is further argument for there being many factors necessary to legitimise an accusation of witchcraft, and that such criteria had not been met convincingly in the eyes of the patriarch of the Nutter family at that time.[72]

What of the accused and their belief or otherwise in their own powers? Although the possibility of leading questions from the justices and judges cannot be dismissed, it has also been suggested that, despite this, 'Many of those whom Nowell's investigations uncovered did consider themselves witches.'[73] In the case of Alizon Device this is particularly striking; it appears she believed without doubt that she was responsible for the suffering of John Law.[74] It also seems clear that both Demdike and Chattox believed themselves capable of the witchcraft of which they were accused. Again, although this seems fantastical to modern readers, in the cultural and religious context of the time, belief in the existence of demons and magic was integral, and from there it was only a short leap to the belief that one could personally affect others in such a way.

Another intriguing aspect of the 1612 case is debate surrounding the origins of the accusations against the accused. The generally accepted theory is that it was the complaint of Abraham Law regarding Alizon Device bewitching his father that led to the devastating result at the Lancaster Assizes in the summer of 1612. This, in turn, allowed Nowell to take action against those who had been bothering the local community for some time.[75] It has also been suggested that it was either 'blatant boasts of enormities, or perhaps the imaginary fears of the neighbours' that reached Nowell's ears, causing him to investigate and act accordingly. The idea that the families themselves were to blame through their 'boasting' and the rivalry between them is common, with the suggestion that 'their enmity to each other and to most of their neighbours culminated in a trial in which one family destroyed the other and then turned suicidally on itself, children betraying siblings and parents.'[76]

Straying from the conventional argument, Walter Bennett offers the interpretation that it was actually the robbery at the Device house that was the beginning of the whole sorry saga. Chattox's younger daughter Bessie (only mentioned once throughout the entirety of Potts's pamphlet account) was responsible for the robbery, and after being accused by Alizon and Elizabeth Device, was arrested and imprisoned. In turn, Bessie spoke out against the Devices regarding witchcraft in order to get her revenge and, overawed and confused, Alizon Device spoke far too much when questioned by Nowell and effectively condemned the lot of them.[77]

Religion was, as to be expected at the time, prominent throughout the case and the testimony of those involved. The belief in the power of the bread used for Communion is highlighted in the words of James Device. According to his account, he was told by his grandmother not to swallow the communion bread when he attended church but to keep it under his tongue; he was then to give it to a spirit that would meet him afterwards. It had long been believed that the host was imbued with special powers, giving the individual who held it in their possession magical abilities if used in specific ways.[80] Due to the widespread nature of such belief, as early as 1215 it was decreed by the Lateran Council that both communion bread and the holy water used in the communion service were to be locked away to prevent theft, and it is clear that this continued to be a concern through the following centuries, as the same order was given in the mid-sixteenth century: Cardinal Pole stipulated that the font at Cambridge was to be kept locked to dissuade would-be thieves.[81] In James Device's case, it was a moot point; the young man swallowed the host and was therefore empty-handed when he met the creature his grandmother had told him to watch for.[82]

Due to the all pervading nature of religious belief in the seventeenth century, it is also not a surprise to discover it playing a role in the political aspect of the Lancashire case, and the timing of the trial has both political and religious significance. Taking place less than a decade after the foiled attempt of Guy Fawkes and his fellow Catholic conspirators to blow up the King and the Houses of Parliament, events were very much still alive in popular memory, and the parallels and similarities in the plan to blow up Lancaster Castle by the associates of Demdike and Chattox would have been immediately apparent.[83] Did the conspirators at Malkin Tower decide to blow up the castle in emulation of the failed attempt on Parliament, taking the earlier and infamous event as inspiration for their own plan to rescue their friends and relations? A discerning reader might question whether the reference made to gunpowder and its intended use was an accurate relation of what was said by those questioned, or whether instead it reflects more the discourse and concerns of Nowell and other members of the elite.[84] Indeed it has been suggested that there was in fact a dual purpose to Potts's writing the pamphlet account of the case – not only was he writing against witches, but also against Catholics, dual threats to both social order and religious and political stability that could not be ignored. One could also speculate whether mention of blowing up the castle was an actual plan, or a mere expression of wishful thinking, an idea voiced in the heat of the moment, never intended to be carried out.[83]

Although the social and economic status of the accused was low, as was generally the case in English witch trials, there is one notable exception often cited with regard to the trial of the Pendle witches. Although Alice Nutter, a widow of around 70 years of age, went to the gallows with Chattox, Alizon Device and the rest, it is widely held that unlike the poverty-stricken majority, she was of a higher standing both socially and financially than those with whom she was condemned. Potts makes it clear in his account that Alice had no need of the riches and other temptations held out by the Devil, and she has been variously described as either a gentlewoman, or from a family of a 'middling sort'.[84] This poses a problem for both Potts and later commentators, as Alice noticeably lacked the potential financial motivation of the others when it came to turning to a life of witchcraft. By nature, Alice was also far from a promising candidate; she had 'children of good hope; in the common opinion of the world, of good temper, free from envy or malice.'[85] Wanting for nothing both in goods or personality then, what brought this apparently unlikely witch before the courts and, from there, to the gallows?

Although it has been suggested that Nowell had a personal reason to want to bring Alice down after a dispute over a law suit, this does not stand up under scrutiny, and also suggests a misunderstanding of the financial implications of being found guilty of witchcraft. Although common in areas of Europe where either magistrates or victims stood to gain from the execution of a witch through taking over their property and any wealth they might have, in England there was little to no financial gain to be made; both the 1563 and 1604 Witchcraft Acts were at pains to safeguard the inheritance a condemned witch might leave behind, however paltry. Also it has been proven that Alice was not quite as rich as she is sometimes made out to be; she was not, for instance, the mistress of Rough Lee Hall as is often maintained and it is likely that her riches have been greatly exaggerated.[86]

Religious considerations are also used to explain Alice's presence in the group, and it has been suggested that she might have been on her way to an illicit Catholic gathering after stopping at Malkin Tower to see if she could help her friend Demdike. Knowing the danger such an admission would put her in, Alice refused to disclose the true purpose of her being out and about that night, with the resultant tragic consequences.[87]

Whatever Alice's reason for being at Malkin Tower, her presence there was enough: Jennet Device had seen her at the meeting and identified her from the group of suspects, and James Device spoke of how he heard Demdike say that Alice Nutter had been instrumental in the death of Henry Mitton. When Elizabeth Device confessed that she, her mother and Alice Nutter had bewitched the man, Alice was condemned with the rest. Unlike most of the Pendle witches, the location of the final resting place of Alice Nutter is believed to be known: a grave in the churchyard of Newchurch-in-Pendle is said to be hers, and can be visited today.[88]

Perhaps more than any other English witch trial (save perhaps those carried out by Matthew Hopkins) the Pendle Witches have captured popular imagination and interest. The personalities and individuals are brought alive, but also created anew each time. The case is still greatly remembered in the area where they lived and died today, and there are many homages to them in Lancaster and beyond, with annual commemorations of what is now seen as a great miscarriage of justice. Interestingly, unlike some areas where there is perhaps a lingering shame over events, the past is remembered, celebrated and embraced so that Chattox, Demdike and their families will never be forgotten. Perhaps the two most famous memorials to the Pendle Witches are in the form of two novels: Harrison Ainsworth's 1849 *The Lancashire Witches*, and *Mist Over Pendle*, written a century later by Robert Neill and published in 1951.[89] These fictionalised accounts have done much to shape and create the image of the Pendle Witches in the popular imagination, resulting in the blend of historical fact and speculative fiction that most people know today.[90] Ultimately, not only does their story provide a chilling reminder of the power of gossip and false testimony, but it also marked the beginning of a century that heralded even worse travesties to come.

Chapter 4

The Witch-Finders: Bury St Edmunds – 1645

> For first the Devil's policy is great, in persuading many to
> come of their own accord to be tried, persuading them their
> marks are so close they shall not be found out, so as diverse
> have come 10 or 12 miles to be searched of their own
> accord, and hanged for their labour.
>
> *The Discovery of Witches*, Matthew Hopkins, 1647

Unlike Continental Europe, there was only one time during its history when England could be said to have experienced a true 'witch craze' or panic.[1] In the mid-seventeenth century, when the country was battling against itself in civil war, the people of England found themselves with another enemy within to contend with: the witch.

The period saw an eruption of accusations and executions for the crime of witchcraft, and the area to suffer the most in this fresh wave of persecution were the towns and villages of East Anglia. With both Suffolk and neighbouring Essex a hotbed of political, social and religious tensions, the area was a smouldering powder keg waiting to explode at any moment. The preceding decades had seen relatively few official accusations for witchcraft, with prosecution and execution on the wane, but now, in the heightened atmosphere of the Civil War and the perceived collapse of order and security, local fears and suspicions that had been building steadily were vented, bubbling over with fatal consequences.

Of all the names connected with this period there are surely none better known than those of Matthew Hopkins and his co-worker John Stearne. With thousands of deaths and horrifying feats of torture and torment attributed to the pair, the 'Witch-Finder General' and his reign of terror are, to many, the epitome of seventeenth-century fanaticism and persecution. Over a period of just three years, Hopkins and Stearne travelled between many towns and villages, identifying and ousting witches in vast numbers as they went. Ensuring that as many victims as possible paid the penalty for their crimes, they themselves were also paid, some said very handsomely, for their work.[2]

One of the largest yields achieved by the witch-finders – and indeed of the entire period – took place at the assizes in the Suffolk town of Bury St Edmunds in August 1645. As related in the pamphlet *A True Relation of the Arraignment of Eighteen Witches that were tried, convicted and condemned, at a Sessions holden at Edmunds-bury in Suffolk,* eighteen individuals from the surrounding area went to the noose as a result of the trial, making it not only a record for Hopkins, but also marking the largest single trying of witches to take place in England.

Their work in Suffolk was not their first; in the early months of 1645, the two men had passed through Essex, leaving a string of suspected witches festering in the foetid conditions of Colchester Castle. They had been rather over-zealous and complaints began to mount, with the pair finally having to leave the county before they were hounded out all together.

With this previous experience as a warning and with a new careful honing of their approach, Hopkins and Stearne had set to work in the neighbouring county of Suffolk: splitting the area between the two of them they made their way through the towns and villages, focusing on those they suspected would be most receptive to them, with encouraging results.

More convinced than ever of the righteousness of their cause, over the summer of 1645 the witch-finders moved from area to area, hearing accusations and apprehending suspects, with confessions and counter accusations extracted from those only too happy to air their long-held grievances about their neighbours. In Chattisham, Anne Alderman and Mary and Nathanial Bacon were implicated in devilish pacts and the owning of imps, as was Rebecca Morris. Individuals from nearby Copdock and Hintlesham were also routed out, adding to the growing list of those implicated in a widening conspiracy of diabolical connections.[3]

Likewise, Jane Linstead 'freely confessed' that she had three imps; they sucked at her frequently, but this did not cause her any pain. One of them she used to upset the work of a baker. Another, more seriously, she sent to kill the daughter of a man named Clarke. The Devil had come to her in the form of a man, and wanted to lie with her; when she refused he was very angry, but despite making threats, he had not hurt her.

Fantastical as such claims might seem, these incidents were neither recent nor peculiar in the area; one old woman who confessed and was condemned stated she had been a witch for over fifty years, during which time she had committed such crimes as bewitching the cattle and crops of her neighbours. The same woman confessed that she had been the cause of death of no less than seven members of the same family, bewitching a couple and their five children through her imps.

Another told those who questioned her that she had been a witch for over twenty-five years and was guilty of bewitching a child to death. She had also meddled with the local cattle, causing death and lameness in the animals, and poverty to their owners as a result. Likewise she had tampered with crops, ruining the corn so that those who owned it would get no money for their labour.

One witch said she had a grudge against a man and his wife who lived in Suffolk. They were annoyed at her coming to their house regularly, and asked her to stop doing so. She took offence at this and had accordingly sent one of her imps in the form of a black dog to distract their son, the couple's only child. Although the boy was cautious around the animal to start with, after persistent visits, the child eventually began to play with it – with disastrous consequences. Seeing its advantage, the dog led the child towards the water, where the boy fell in and drowned.

Arrests were made by the dozen, the numbers held to await the next assizes swelling the already overcrowded prisons. All confessed to bewitching many men, women and children to death. Also horses, oxen, cows, sheep and other livestock, along with corn, herbs and plants. Likewise, they raised storms to damage and destroy buildings, haystacks, trees – striking at the very things that would cause most hurt to those against whom they sought revenge. The majority of those that confessed stated that envy and malice were behind their actions, and that they had all made a covenant or pact with the Devil who had appeared to them several times before they had taken the final, irredeemable step.

Another thing held in common by the accused was that, when searched, most were found to have teats on their bodies, used by the imps to suck from and a sure sign that they had made a pact with the Devil. They were in different locations – generally hidden – such as under an arm, under a tongue, hidden on the roof of the suspect's mouth, or between their toes. They came in various sizes but were generally small, and there were reports of some shaped like thunderbolts, another clue as to their 'unnatural' origin. The imps themselves came in a variety of forms, most commonly as animals such as mice, kittens, snails, snakes, hornets and wasps.

Thus were the confessions and physical signs of the many women and several men who found themselves questioned under suspicion of being witches in the area that fateful summer. The sheer volume of the accused and the increasingly crowded conditions of the prisons and other places used to hold suspects awaiting the summer Assizes was unprecedented, and the advance of the Cavalier army in August lent further urgency to proceedings; on twenty-fourth of that month, royalist forces took the nearby town of Huntingdon, during which, amidst great violence, the prisons were emptied and prisoners set free. In the early hours of the following day the alarm was raised that troops were approaching Bury St Edmunds itself.

Despite, or perhaps because of, the advancing threat, the first trial of witchcraft suspects took place at Bury St Edmunds on Tuesday 26 August. Eighteen people were condemned, sentenced to die the following day, the need for speed of turnaround between trial and resolution never more pressing.

Amongst the condemned was Reverend John Lowes, the vicar of Brandeston. Lowes confessed to making a pact with the Devil, after which he had continued to preach to his congregation with impunity. Not content with this he had bewitched a ship near Harwich, raising such storms and tempests that the ship, filled with passengers, was tossed out to sea, causing the death of all those on board. Lowes had also confessed to carrying out many other horrendous acts with the help of the six imps that worked for him and did his bidding. This was far from suspicion and hearsay; physical proof existed of Lowes's wretched state. The diabolically influenced rector had a teat on the top of his head and two under his tongue, stark evidence of the deadly covenant he had made.

Thomas Everard, a cooper by trade, along with his wife Mary, were also found guilty. The couple worked in a brew house in Halfworth, Suffolk, and had bewitched the beer there. This poisoned beer had caused the deaths of several people, and the couple had also caused other mischief to people of their choosing through the use of imps, including the death of their own grandchild. According to the pamphlet, the rest of the condemned were Mary Bacon, Anne Alderman, Rebecca Morris, Mary Fuller, Mary Clowes, Margery Sparham, Katherine Teoney, Sarah Spinlow, Jane Linstead, Anne Wright, Mary Smith, Jane River, Susan Manners, Mary Skinner and Anne Leech.

After their fate was decided the group were held in a barn in the town, kept apart from those who were yet to face trial.[4] There is some indication of the mood of the condemned as they gathered together during that long, final night. Far from despairing, it seems they united in a final show of defiance; it was said that the prisoners made a pact not to confess anything further than they had said already, to go to the gallows in silence, despite whatever they might have said before. Only one of their number refused to agree to this arrangement. With the matter decided the condemned said prayers and sang together before settling to sleep as best they could until morning.

When dawn came, as agreed, the condemned kept their vow of silence. The woman who had abstained from making the promise with the rest was equally true to her word; unlike her companions she was anything but quiet, railing against her fellow prisoners all the way to the scaffold. In doing so she revealed the pact along with her rejection of it, making it clear to all who could hear that she had no part in the agreement.[5] The hangman did his work and all differences ceased to matter: eighteen more names added to the witch hunters' death toll.

Of the two men responsible for this latest tragedy, John Stearne at least appears to have been in attendance at the execution as he made mention of several details in his later writings. It is unclear whether Matthew Hopkins was present, but their role in events does not appear to have troubled the conscience of either man – quite the contrary, in fact. They were, after all, doing God's work, ridding the country of those who had given themselves to the Devil.

Out of necessity rather than scruples the bloodshed was put on hold; the assize court adjourned for the space of three weeks due to the Royalist threat that could no longer be ignored. When it finally reconvened, the second sitting yielded yet more condemnations, though it is not clear just how many men and women were executed before the fever of prosecution finally abated.[6]

****

There is no denying that the execution of the eighteen suspected witches in August 1645 played a crucial role in the history of the area, carving a niche both politically and socially and shaping this prominent period in England's witchcraft history. According to John Stearne, the death-toll was much higher; by his reckoning, sixty-eight were eventually condemned 'all at one gaol delivery' in the summer of that year, and he claimed a staggering 200 had been executed in that area since May.[7]

Although the largest, this was not the first witchcraft case to come before the Bury St Edmund's assizes; three women were tried as far back as 1599. In that year, Joan Jordan and Joan Nayler from Shadbrooke in Suffolk were apparently tried, though it is not clear for what, or what became of the two women.[8] Olive Barthram intriguingly was also tried and found guilty of sending spirits to torment, presumably the same, Joan Jordan. These spirits were in the form of toads, and there was much carry-on to remove them from the house, resulting in Joan being 'violently thrown down' in the attempt. It was also testified by several people that Olive sent a further spirit in the form of a cat named Gyles, who,

> came now again at 11 o'clock at night, first scraping on the walls, then knocking ... he clapped the maid on the cheeks about a half score times as to awake her ... kissed her three or four times, and slavered on her, and (lying on her breast) he pressed her so sore that she could not speak.[9]

Neither would the 1645 trials be the last time accusations of witchcraft darkened the Suffolk assizes: in 1664 Rose Cullender and Amy Duny, both from Lowestoft, were accused of bewitching seven children and causing great misery and suffering to those they tormented. With a huge amount of 'evidence' given against them, the two young women were tragically found guilty and executed.

The Bury St Edmunds trial is of particular note for many reasons, one of which is that one of the main targets was not a woman as was so often the case when it came to witchcraft accusations, but a man. John Lowes had been minister of his parish for fifty years, and during that time he had attracted much in the way of censure, his downfall at the hands of Hopkins a classic and brutal example of how witch-belief and the trial process could be used to advance local agendas and remove those who were seen as problematic or disliked.

As with so many accusations involving witchcraft, the Lowes case has a long backstory, which is instructive when making sense of the unfortunate minister's eventual fate. The Suffolk village of Brandeston, of which Lowes had been vicar since 1595, had a population of about 100 people during the mid-seventeenth century.[10] Like several clergy members of the period, Lowes came under suspicion during the conflict of the Civil War when, suspected of Popish and therefore Royalist leanings, he was labelled 'scandalous', believed to be presenting a direct challenge to the reigning model of Puritanism. Men in Lowes's position were considered particularly dangerous due to the authority and influence they were seen to have over those to whom they preached, and one of the complaints against him was the influence he was said to have over the minds of the younger members of his parish. Furthermore, Lowes's style of preaching, along with his manipulation of tithe payments, caused a great deal of resentment, and he most certainly did not endear himself to his parishioners when, with the pulpit and chancel in the church in a bad condition, he not only had them repaired to be more in line with his own design taste, but also made sure that the parish footed the bill.[11] Lowes also had a reputation for action, and on several occasions took out law suits against those who slandered or acted against him, something else that did little for his already poor reputation.[12]

As early as 1615, a yeoman named Jonas Cooke testified against Lowes at Woodbridge Quarter Sessions, asserting that the minister was a 'common barretor' – i.e. someone who had fraudulent dealings – and disturber of the peace. Lowes countered with an appeal to the Court of King's Bench in London, emerging triumphant against Cooke and his fellow detractors. Although he was successful in evading prosecution at Woodbridge, it was not long before the unpopular minister was named again at the sessions; this time it was due to his intervention when local woman Ann Ansom was accused of witchcraft by some of his parishioners – including Jonas Cooke. Lowes took the poor woman's side, the tenacity and conviction for which he was known and derided leaving him unable to remain silent in face of what he considered to be wrong. Ansom was, Lowes declared, no more a witch than he was himself – words that would soon be twisted and used against him by those who wanted nothing more than to see him brought down. Furthermore, Lowes gave the persecuted woman shelter within his own home whilst those who accused her made threats outside. Whatever his motivation for helping Ansom, Lowes was temporarily thwarted as she was forcibly removed from his house and committed on suspicion of witchcraft. Even then Lowes refused to let the matter drop; after threatening Jonas Cook and his associates, the vilified minister persuaded his own brother to organise the woman's bail.

The incident didn't end well; despite Lowes's efforts, in February 1615 Ann Ansom was indicted for the murder of John May by witchcraft, those siding with Cooke testifying gleefully against her: she was found guilty and hanged.[13] What should have been the tragic end of the matter proved to be only the beginning. Livestock belonging to several witnesses in the case began to fall sick and die, and it was not long before the finger of suspicion was firmly pointed at Ansom's staunchest supporter: John Lowes.

Matters grew progressively more hostile, culminating in Lowes being charged with, but declared innocent of, various crimes: causing the death of Mary Cooke (daughter to Jonas), helping Ann Ansom destroy cattle, and poisoning the son of a gentleman from Framlingham.[14]

Despite this victory, the conflict between Lowes and Cooke continued to simmer along over the following decades, occasionally spilling over into the courts. Finally, frustrated at the lack of official action taken against Lowes, in 1645 Cooke and his associates went to the lengths of producing a pamphlet against the controversial prelate: *A Magazine of Scandal*, which purported to reveal 'A heape of wickedness of two infamous Ministers, consorts, one named Thomas Fowkes … convicted by law for killing a man, and the other named John Lowes of Brandeston, who hath be arraigned for witchcraft, and convicted by law for a common burretor.'[15] Not only that, the two men were, according to the account, 'the head and most notorious of the scandalous ministers within the County of Suffolk, and well may be said of all England.'[16]

According to the pamphlet the two men were responsible for cheating their parishioners out of money in a variety of ways, exploiting tithes and helping each other to line their own pockets in the process. Lowes especially, of 'pragmatic disposition' and 'nimble as a dancer', was tricksy, cunning and manipulative.[17] Considering himself something of a lawyer, with a good knowledge of not only spiritual but also common law, the minister was accused of using this greatly to his advantage; taking it upon himself to help many in their business, Lowes tended to put himself in the position of arbitrator between two parties, and, after taking money from both sides, declaring for whoever had paid him the most. In this way, it was declared, Lowes had 'advised many to their undoing', ultimately looking only to his own best interests.[18]

Another crime heaped upon Lowes and his co-conspirator was a reputation for showing little constancy when it came to religion, blowing whichever way best suited their own interests at any given time.[19] They were particularly fond of those with Catholic leanings, and 'both daily have frequented the company of known popish recusants.'[20]

Where the topic of witchcraft is concerned, the author likewise doesn't mince words, declaring that 'This barretor ... hath been so vehemently suspected of witchcraft, that he hath been twice indicted, and once arraigned for witchcraft.' Aware that there might be those who quibbled with this accusation, it goes on further to point out that: 'Whether it be so or not, it is most certain that many have so accused him upon their deaths, and it is most certain that he hath used the society and help of those that have been convicted and executed for witchcraft.'[21] Not only was Lowes guilty of witchcraft himself therefore, he had also used the services of other witches to achieve his nefarious aims. There was, apparently, nothing Lowes was not capable of; a further accusation against the minister was that he had threatened to burn the houses around the ears of his parishioners if they were successful in evicting him from his post![22]

Despite Cooke's consistently thwarted attempts to rid the area of Lowes and the concerted efforts of several other parishioners, it was not until 1645 itself that the threat of the noose became real. Margery Chimery, held in Framlingham for witchcraft, told Matthew Hopkins himself that Lowes had visited and warned her not to confess anything on the matter of witchcraft. This was taken as evidence that Lowes was in fact the head of the dangerous sect of witches that were running rife in the area, and one of the most dangerous individuals involved in the whole affair.

The now elderly man was arrested and pressed to confess; despite being 'walked' and kept awake, Lowes – as further proof of his resolute nature – refused to incriminate himself. The wily minister had met his match; however Hopkins had him taken to Framlingham Castle, his own family seat, where he was unceremoniously swum in the ditch there. How deep the water was or what the conditions were like was not recorded, but Lowes floated and was therefore pronounced guilty.[23]

With further people coming forward to accuse him and his continued ill-treatment – it was recorded that 'the watchers kept the old man awake several nights together, and ran him backwards and forwards about the room, until he was breathless ... weary of his life and scarce sensible of what he said or did,' Lowes finally cracked and began to confess as required.[24] After making his pact with the Devil, he told Hopkins, he had allowed his three familiars to suck from him and had caused much harm by sea and land, most notably the sinking of a brand new ship near Harwich.

Taken before the magistrate, his evidence was recorded, and Lowes was sent to gaol in Ipswich to await the assizes at Bury St Edmunds. When it came to his turn in court, despite taking back his previous confession, Lowes was convicted and condemned to die.[25] Despite the final pact of silence made between the condemned, Lowes had one final request: to be allowed to conduct his own funeral service by reciting from the Book of Common Prayer before he was turned off. Permitted to do so, it can be hoped that this brought some comfort at least to the man who was now in his eighties; it was, to his detractors, only seen as further proof of Lowes's ungodliness and un-puritan ways.

Even after the executions, interest in the notorious Lowes did not fade. There was talk that he had claimed to have a charm that would protect him from hanging (Stearne referred self-righteously to the fact in his 1648 pamphlet three years later, stating Lowes 'had a charm to keep him out of gaol, and hanging, as he paraphrased it himself, but therein the Devil deceived him; for he was hanged.')[26] Thomas Ady opined in his 1655 publication, *Candle in the Dark*, that the accusations made against Lowes were preposterous, and that the winds said to have been raised by him would have been miraculous even for Christ. Several other fantastical claims were attributed to him in the years following his death and his fate was of particular interest to Francis Hutchinson – later author of the influential *An Historical Essay Concerning Witchcraft* – during his time as curate at Bury.[27]

The 'scandalous' minister of Brandeston has captured and held popular imagination throughout the ages, both in his own right, and also in what he represents: the barbarous treatment and death of the innocent.

Another area where the trial at Bury St Edmunds stands out is regarding potential methods used to obtain confessions from suspects. Yes, the condemned had confessed, but under what conditions? Despite being rife on the Continent and used there to extract many confessions during the period of the witch trials, torture, in the purely legal sense of the term, was against the law in seventeenth-century England.[28] This oft-quoted fact is somewhat misleading, and the mention that an accused witch 'confessed freely' could have more connotations than at first meets the eye. The pamphlet account of the Bury St Edmunds trial itself outlines the process of finding and then obtaining a confession from a suspect:

> There are in the County of Suffolk four searchers appointed
> for the finding of them out, two men searchers and two women
> searchers, the men are to search those men who are suspected

to be witches, and the women searchers likewise are to search those women that are supposed to be witches ... thither they send for two or all of the said searchers, who take the party or parties so suspected into a room and strip him, her, or them, stark naked, and on whom the searchers find any teats or dugs, that party or parties, the said searchers set upon a stool or stools, in the midst of the room, so that the feet of him, her or them, may not touch the ground. Nevertheless the party or parties may sometimes walk up and down the said room, so that there be sure watch kept, that none of his, her, or their familiar imps come at him, her or them.[29]

Although not 'torture' in the legal sense of the word, it was a far cry from what, in modern terms, would be counted as confessing 'freely', and such claims must therefore be approached with caution. If the definition of treatment was a tricky one, the justification given for keeping watch for the appearance of familiars was simple by contrast; if the accused was indeed a witch, within twenty-four hours the imps would have to come to be fed; if they did not, the witch would be in great physical torment which would be another tangible sign of his or her guilt.

The direct result of such treatment, whatever the reasoning behind it, was that in practice, those suspected of witchcraft were deprived of sleep for long periods of time and forced to walk up and down by 'watchers' in order to keep them awake. As anyone who has found themselves unable to sleep for even one night can testify, sleep deprivation can cause great mental and physical strain; with many of the accused kept from sleep for several days on end, it is easy to imagine how a suspect could be driven to admit to almost anything in order to obtain some respite.

The pamphlet account and other sources make it clear that the practices of walking and 'waking' were far from uncommon. Rebecca Morris stood out as having confessed 'before any violence, watching or other threats', a references that strongly suggests that voluntary confession without any intervention was not the norm, or at least far enough removed from it to be worth mentioning.[30] Direct references to the length of time suspects were watched for are likewise littered throughout the depositions recorded; Susan Manners of Copdock was watched from Monday until Wednesday when she confessed that her grandmother had given her two imps, whilst Anne Marsh was watched for two days and two nights, during which time she threatened those watching her that she would get her revenge on them. Tragically in the case of Anne Marsh, one of her watchers had left two small children behind at home with an open fire; as can be imagined this was a recipe for disaster, and one child burned to death, the tragedy seen as vengeance from the witch herself.[31] John Chambers likewise made his confession after three days of being watched.[32]

There is a great deal of evidence regarding contemporary belief in familiars in the documents relating to the Bury St Edmund's trial, both on a popular and academic level, and the differences between the two can be illuminating. It is clear for instance that the names of these imps or spirits as confessed by the accused themselves were mostly 'human' sounding names, the sort they would use for pets or people. However, both Hopkins and Stearne report decidedly more outlandish names in their accounts, with Hopkins gleefully listing those such as 'Elemanzer, Pyewacket, Peckin the Crown, Grizzel Greedigut etc, which no mortal could invent,' likely in an attempt to add further credence to their claims.[33]

The different shapes and forms these familiars or imps could take were numerous. Cats, poultry, toads, ferrets, and a variety of insects are mentioned both in the words of the accused and by the witch hunters themselves. These familiars could also change shape: Joan Ruce of Powstead in Suffolk related how, after she had made her pact with the Devil, 'there appeared in a bush things like chickens, about five or six, and that she had catched three of them … and that she carried them home, which soon after turned to the likeness of mice.'[34]

Most intriguingly, both Stearne and Hopkins claimed to have seen some of these 'imps' themselves during the times they watched and questioned suspects. Stearne relates how Elizabeth Clarke told himself and Hopkins that if they stayed in the room she would show them her imps. Having caught their attention, Elizabeth proceeded to call a name and the first imp appeared in the form of a cat, just as she had predicted. Another followed not long after, this time in the shape of a red spotted dog 'with legs not so long as a finger … but his back as broad as two dogs, or broader'.[35] Thus came a steady procession of Elizabeth's familiars, seven or eight in total. Elizabeth Clarke then apparently went on to threaten Stearne, saying that the next imp to appear would tear him to pieces. When asked why, she informed him that it was because he had wanted to swim her and this was her chance to get even. It would come in the shape of a black toad, and indeed it did appear, though it is unclear whether Stearne himself witnessed this or just those who were with him.[36]

The presence of marks or teats on the bodies of the accused and the methods of discovering said marks were also of great importance to both Stearne and Hopkins, their whole argument in justification of their approach hinging on both their importance and detection. Accordingly, much of both of their pamphlets are taken up with describing what the marks looked like, where they were to be found, and just why they were so crucial to the discovery of a witch, with Stearne declaring that 'Here you may observe, that the diligentness of searching is a great matter, and one of the chiefest points of their [the witches] discovery.'[37] It is a matter that is returned to again and again and seems to have been a particular preoccupation of Stearne's, who avowed that discovering the marks through searching was the most likely way to obtain a confession from a suspect, and was 'both the most ready and certain way, as that if they which undertake it be careful there can be no mistake.'[38] He was also convinced that 'all that have these, or any of these marks, are guilty of witchcraft.'[39]

It was crucial, therefore, that those carrying out the searching were skilled in their task and knew exactly what they were looking for, as it was easy to miss the marks or, in some cases, for the suspect to conceal the teats that would reveal their guilt. Accordingly, searchers needed to be 'able people, of discretion and good carriage', especially as money, by way of bribes, and a lack of knowledge regarding the marks had, sadly, led to guilty parties going free.[40] This was particularly important as those who tried to conceal their marks would go to any lengths to do so, even to the point of removing them physically from their bodies if hiding them by supernatural means did not work, with Stearne warning that: 'Sometimes the flesh is sunk in a hollow, that is, where they pull them off, and pull them out with their nails, or otherwise cause them to be pulled off.'[41] A woman in Cambridgeshire had actually done this, and there were, he had no doubt, many others who resorted to such extreme measures to avoid being caught out.

Another central theme to the beliefs of Hopkins and Stearne was the pact made by suspected witches with the Devil. The Devil was both cunning and subversive, using parodied Christian rituals and practices to gain control over those whose souls he took and also, by extension, getting one over on his heavenly rival. Baptisms, assemblies and covenants were all taken on by the Devil and given a new, terrible meaning, and it was in this way that he managed to coerce many to follow him.

The Devil as a trickster is a common theme throughout English folklore, and his reputation as a liar frequently occurs throughout the confessions recorded at Bury St Edmunds. Of particular note is the number of times the accused claim to have been promised money, only for the Devil to fail to live up to his side of the bargain. The Devil apparently promised Priscilla Collit of Dunwich ten shillings, but the money was never given, and Anne Barker complained of how the Devil had told her where some money was hidden, only for her search to prove fruitless. A rare example of someone benefiting financially from the Devil was Joan Ruce who said she had received four or six shillings on a few occasions, though those were, she admitted, not very often.[42] Stearne himself said that obtaining money from the Devil was rare, and the only other person he could recall actually getting any money to show for the promises was Elizabeth Clarke from Manningtree; he had seen this money with his own eyes, declaring it to be 'perfect' and not counterfeit.[43]

It is also instructive to examine what Hopkins and Stearne believed caused suspects to turn to witchcraft in the first place. According to the witch hunters, those who became witches only did so because they were already in a state of preparedness to welcome the Devil into their lives. It was simply a case of the Devil biding his time, as,

> He therefore watcheth the time when he may best offer his service to such as any way he finds the least kind of preparedness in, as when any fall into a passionate sorrow, accompanied with solitariness for some loss, a husband, wife, children or such like, the Devil offers himself to comfort such in their sorrowful melancholy mood.[44]

Poverty, the desire to be rich, anger, wanting revenge or being prone to associating with those who were already witches also primed a person to be more receptive to the Devil's advances, as was the inclination and habit of reading 'dangerous books'.[45] This again links to the explanation regarding the larger number of women over men who were accused of witchcraft. Women were more likely to lose a husband than vice versa in the seventeenth century, with the number of widows in proportion to widowers greatly on the increase throughout the period in question. The death of a spouse was believed to be particularly likely to leave a woman open to being seduced – sometimes literally – by the Devil; there are several mentions of women turning to witchcraft shortly after the deaths of their husbands, again reinforcing their weaker nature as opposed to that of men.

In 1645, Thomazine Ratcliffe from Shelley confessed that twenty years earlier, 'soon after' the death of her husband, the Devil came to her in the form of a man, promising to be a good husband to her before entering her bed.[46] Mary Skipper of Copdock likewise admitted that the Devil came to to her after her husband had died, also as a man, and promised to pay her debts – he also gave her three imps.[47] Margery Sparham said that although she had one of her imps before her marriage, two further imps came to her after her father had died and, now married, she sent them to her soldier husband in the hope that he would be protected by them.[48]

Despair in general was present in many of the confessions. With many of the accused coming from the poor (and growing steadily poorer) amongst society, this was not greatly surprising, although the grief and sorrow related in many confessions is heart rending to say the least. Depression, suicidal thoughts and the urge to do harm to their children occur with sobering frequency in the recorded confessions. Ellen Greenlief had contemplated taking her own life on more than one occasion, and Anne Alderman said she had used her imp to kill her own child. Priscilla Collit from Dunwich likewise spoke of how twelve years earlier in 1633, whilst she was unwell, the Devil had tempted her to kill her children. She had placed one before the fire and left it there to burn, the child was only saved by being pulled away from harm by another of her children.[49] Mary Scrutton of Framlingham reported how the Devil had come to her in the shape of a bear and then a cat, urging her to kill her child. The guilt such feelings must have generated in these women, and perhaps had done for some time, now had a vent in their confessions as they admitted them out loud; it was an unburdening that came at great cost. Those who harboured ill-feeling towards their spouses likewise thought themselves responsible for any ill that befell them, the causal relationship between ill thoughts and actual outcome being accepted unquestioningly in many cases by both suspect and accuser.[50]

One of the most sensational claims of those questioned by Hopkins and Stearne was that of having sex with the Devil.[51] Most alarmingly, one woman admitted to having conceived twice in this way (before her husband died). The children ran away as soon as they were born, but not before it became apparent that they were horribly deformed. Mary Bacon confessed that she had lain with the Devil, and that he was 'cold'.[52] Margaret Bennett from Bacton claimed that 'the Devil in a long cloak' carried her into a thicket and lay with her, whilst Anne Cricke, a widow of Hitcham, said he had used her body but, intriguingly, that she 'could not tell whether he performed nature or not'.[53]

This element makes the confessions at Bury St Edmunds and others of the Hopkins period stand out, as sexual intercourse with the Devil was more notably a staple of Continental witch trials and not commonplace in England. It is thought that a combination of leading questions, in turn influenced by the reading of the writings of European scholars and witch hunters were responsible for such sensational elements appearing in English witchcraft narratives, providing a useful insight into the divide and overlap between popular and learned belief of the time.

Another prevalent belief regarding witchcraft during the Hopkins period was that it did not occur in isolation. Witchcraft was believed to run in families, passed down from one generation to the next by word of mouth and practical instruction. This belief was reflected in the confessions of several who were questioned before the Bury St Edmund trial; Rebecca West was, according to Stearne, 'drawn to it by her mother', and confessed how her mother had taken her to Manningtree, telling her on the way that if she did not speak of what would occur there she would be 'a happy woman'.[54] Susan Manners of Copdock confessed that she had received her two imps from her grandmother.[55] It was testified that the mother of Elizabeth Man of Wickham had been hanged as a witch, and that Elizabeth in turn had caused the death of a child and the illness of a woman through her own witchcraft.[56] It was not only women who could be thus implicated; Alexander Sussums of Melford told how his mother and aunt were hanged for witchcraft and his grandmother burned, and he therefore could not help likewise following in their footsteps.[57]

The passing of imps to friends and associates was also common, again taking place between women either in the same town or village or spreading further afield. Anne Leech (an accused witch executed in Essex under the reign of Hopkins and Stearne prior to the Bury St Edmund's Trial, but included in the pamphlet account of that case) had confessed that thirty years earlier she had been given a white imp, a grey imp and a black imp by Anne Pearce, the wife of Robert Pearce from Stoke. Since that time she, along with Elizabeth Clarke and Elizabeth Gooding, had sent their imps to kill a black cow and a white cow belonging to a Mr Edwards. Not only that, she and Elizabeth Gooding had each sent an imp to kill Edwards's child. Anne also confessed that she had sent her grey imp, Elizabeth Clarke's black imp and Elizabeth Gooding's white imp to Mr Bragge of Mistley, to likewise kill two of his horses. This was not entirely without provocation; Mistress Bragge had opined that she, Anne, was a 'naughty woman'.[58] She was also aware that Elizabeth Gooding had sent an imp to torment Mary Taylor, wife of John Taylor of Manningtree about three years earlier, the cause being that Mary had refused to give her beer. As little as eight weeks earlier, she, Elizabeth Gooding and Anne West (widow) of Lawford had met together at Elizabeth Clarke's house; during this meeting, a book had been read, and although she could not say what it contained, she was certain it was not a good one.[59] The firm belief in both the familial and community nature of witchcraft in this way heightened and ensured the spread of accusations that took place throughout Essex and Suffolk under Hopkins and Stearne and can be seen as one of the factors responsible for the 'witch hunt' that resulted.[60]

One thing that cannot be doubted about Hopkins and Stearne is their firm conviction that witches deserved death. Witches had existed since biblical times, and the two men saw themselves as duty-bound and charged with the task of routing out such evil and the threat they posed, as, 'All that be in open league with the Devil ought to die.'[61] The justification for this was also biblical, with Stearne asserting that this came, 'First, from God in the giving of his law against witches. Thou Shalt not suffer a witch to live, which implyeth a discovery of them, else it could never be put in execution, and so should be a law to no purpose.'[62]

Despite the vehemence of the witch-finders, there were those who survived their ordeal. Elizabeth Warne was one of those fortunates; she was walked and kept awake until she confessed to having the Devil in her and ended up in court. A month later she is recorded in her home town of Framlingham again and died there many years later.[63]

After the noose, the second biggest cause of death of those suspected of witchcraft was the state they were held in both before and after trial. Across the country, the conditions that the accused were kept in whilst awaiting trial were far from sanitary, and it is probable that several of those whose trials were postponed due to the approaching royalist army in 1645 cheated the noose due to dying in prison before they could come before the courts.[64] Stearne records, regarding a man named Cherrie from Northamptonshire, that, 'This Cherrie confessed presently after he was searched, who died at Northampton in the Gaol there, the same day he should have been tried.'[65] In a case in Chelmsford in July 1645, four of those to be tried died beforehand.[66]

That Hopkins and Stearne acted as though they had authority to carry out their work is not in question. What, if any, authorisation had they actually been granted? In Essex, Stearne was granted what he termed a 'warrant ... for the searching of such persons as I should nominate'.[67] This was from a local official, and not the wide-reaching authority that many believed the pair to possess, and whether or not this first document would cover the pair in Suffolk was doubtful.[68] Despite the rumour that they had been given wider authority by Parliament, there is in fact no surviving evidence of this having been the case, and the reasoning behind their confidence and movements must continue to be speculative. Indeed, questions and concerns were being raised in the areas visited by Hopkins and Stearne as early as the year of the Bury St Edmunds trial. These misgivings had reached official ears, and a Special Commission of Oyer and Terminer, headed by Serjeant Godbold and Edmund Calamy, had been established to make sure that proper procedure was followed during the trial itself. As a gauge of which way the wind was blowing, two sermons were preached by Samuel Fairclough; the first against witchcraft in general, whilst the second spoke out specifically against false and violent prosecution. The warnings against both were also repeated by Godbold to the trial Jury, with the additional reminder that although confessions were supposed to be obtained voluntarily, rumours had reached them that this was not the case and therefore they should take this into consideration when listening to the evidence put before them.

The Moderate Intelligencer news sheet for 4–11 September 1645, likewise expressed unease with how affairs were being conducted and the results of the 'confessions' being obtained, wondering 'but whence it is that Devils should choose to be conversant with silly women that know not their right hands from their left, is the great wonder.'[69] Indeed, if the Devil were as wise and powerful as he was purported to be, why were he and his minions not influencing princes and generals to great feats of evil instead of helping women with the petty killing of geese and pigs and hens and children and contenting himself with the meddling of 'poor old women'?[70]

That there were such grumblings about their methods, Hopkins and Stearne were only too aware. By 1647 the self-styled witch-finder had a pamphlet published to address the increasing criticisms that were being levelled against him and his fellow associates amidst rising complaints about the worst excesses of their work. *The Discovery of Witches* is set out in question and answer format, providing a telling list of the biggest complaints against Hopkins and his fellow witch-finder, John Stearne.

The practice of keeping a suspect awake was one of the first to be addressed. Hopkins asserted that his use of this method dated from his first personal experience of dealing with witches, which came only the year before the Bury St Edmunds trial took place.[71] In this case, the Justice had ordered the woman be kept awake for two to three nights in order to give her familiars time to visit and therefore prove her witchery. Sure enough, on the fourth night the woman called the imps by their names and also revealed what shape they would take; the spirits accordingly appeared, exactly as she had described them and thus cemented her guilt. Endorsed by authority, Hopkins, as he was quick to point out, could hardly be held to blame for the adoption of the practice into his own work. In further justification he went on to relate how waking had proved a useful tool by magistrates in Essex and Suffolk, as being kept awake meant the witch was more likely to call for her familiars which would then provide the proof of her guilt all the sooner. Not only that, he assured readers '… and never or seldom did any witch ever complain in the time of their keeping for want of rest.'[72] Stearne also insisted that the point of watching was not to do violence towards those who were suspected or to force them to confess – it was simply to see whether the 'witch's' familiar spirits would come to them and thus prove their league with the Devil.[73] Either way, the protest against waking was indeed a moot point; Stearne had not used the method for a good year and a half, after the order came to desist in it.[74]

Hopkins was likewise quick to deny culpability when it came to the matter of walking a suspect. This was not a simple matter of just leading a suspect up and down the room in which they were held; in practice, the constant movement, barefoot over rough flooring, left the soles of the feet raw and bleeding, the agony added to the torment of lack of rest. Although he couldn't deny its usage outright, Hopkins insisted again that it had been carried out with the tacit agreement and permission of local Justices. Not as torture, but to better keep the accused awake and to keep their familiars away, as if they lay or crouched down, the imps would come and not only scare the watchers but also give courage and hearten the witch.[75]

There were some, even Hopkins had to admit in the face of glaring evidence, who might misuse these methods, but he challenged readers to be able to find evidence that he himself was guilty of it as it '…could never be proved against this Discoverer to have a hand in it, or consent to it'.[76] Stearne likewise refuted any knowledge of suspects being kept from food or basic comfort – if they were in 'baser' accommodation than might be desired this was soon rectified once a Justice was in the area, and in most cases the accused actually found themselves in better conditions than they could expect at home.[77] Again as with waking, it was asserted that Hopkins and those working for him had not used the practice for the last eighteen months.

Swimming was another practice that came under fire by their detractors, classed as 'abominable, inhumane and unmerciful', and 'a trial not allowable by law or conscience'.[78] Hopkins again didn't deny that swimming had been used, and also that those with 'paps' often floated whilst those who didn't have them sank, as in keeping with the belief that a witch would be rejected by the water and therefore float. As with everything else, Hopkins stated that this wasn't initiated by him, many actually came of their own accord asking to be swum in order to prove their own innocence, advised by the Devil to do so as, if they got away with it, their guilt would remain unknown. John Stearne again echoed this fact, stating that they never swum anyone but on their own request, and adding that when they did it took place 'at such time of the year as when none took any harm by it', implying that in the summer months the water would have been warmer and therefore less treacherous.[79]

Other criticisms levelled against Hopkins and his methods included the fact that so-called teats and paps could easily be the natural signs of ageing on a body, protests that it was easy to distinguish these from the marks of the Devil particularly unconvincing. Furthermore he was accused of offering mercy to those who confessed and threatening those who did not with the noose and not only that, but of being in league with the Devil himself.[80]

Firmly adhering to his position of blamelessness, Hopkins asserted his belief that a confession was not valid if obtained after torture, and that although confession and execution had taken place after waking, walking and swimming had been carried out, the magistrates involved had been careful to examine the accused after they had slept to make sure they maintained their story before they were convicted.[81] He likewise denied obtaining confessions through false promises or that confessions were valid if leading questions had been asked. Far from it, when a witch was discovered to have teats, she was taken from her home so that she could not continue to mix with her associates in evil, and through 'good counsel' was brought to understand and confess the wickedness of her ways.

The final criticism addressed was that 'all that the Witch-finder doeth, is to fleece the country of their money, and therefore rides and goes to towns to have employment.'[82] Hopkins refuted this categorically, maintaining that he only went where he was asked to go, and that far from making his fortune, he was actually out of pocket a great deal of the time. Providing details to support this claim he assured his readers that he, demands but 20 pounds a town, and does sometimes ride 20 miles for that, and has no more for all his charges there and back again (and it may be stays a week there) and finds there 3 or 4 witches, or if it be but one, cheap enough, and this is the great sum he takes to maintain his company with 3 horses.[83]

Stearne also lamented the lack of remuneration,

Now whosoever thou beest that thinkest I ever made such gain of the way, or favoured any, and persecuted others, or took bribes, I call God to witness, that considering the charge of going to several places, and assizes, and gaol-deliveries, and the time I expended thereabouts, I never, one time with another, got so much as I did by my calling and practice, towards the maintenance of my family.[84]

Despite their protests, it seems that Hopkins and his team were not quite as hard pressed as they made out; accounts for Aldeburgh for instance show that in total they received £6, whilst in Stowmarket they were paid £28 for their work discovering seven witches.[85]

Whatever Hopkins's strident protestations on these issues, his words fell on deaf ears, and his former good reputation continued to wane until popular and official opinion against him made it impossible for the pair to continue with their work. John Stearne retired from public life as 1647 came to a close, but he was not entirely silent, his work *A Confirmation and Discovery of Witchcraft*, building on what Hopkins had already started in his own *Discovery*, justifying their work and refuting the criticisms levelled against them as he maintained the righteousness and necessity of their crusade. It too fell on deaf ears and Stearne was steadfastly remembered long after his death in 1670 for the terrible things they had accomplished.[86] It was clear that the turn of opinion against them greatly chagrined both men and they spent the remainder of their respective lives arguing and shouting against what they felt was the unjust treatment received for their pains.

The fate of Matthew Hopkins himself continues to attract a great deal of attention and speculation, and the legend surrounding this most reviled of figures continues to grow even today. Some say that Hopkins fell victim to his own practices and, suspected as a witch, was swum and found wanting; his life ending, quite justly, on the gallows where he had sent so many other more innocent souls. Another theory holds that Hopkins, knowing his days to be numbered in England, faked his own death before sailing for America to join his brother, where he was influential in the Salem Witch Trials that followed.

As entertaining as such theories are, the rather less exciting but more likely truth is that Hopkins died of tuberculosis in the summer of 1647, not long after the publication of his attempt to justify his witch-finding actions. Stearne himself confirmed that Hopkins died a natural death, stating that: 'I am certain ... he died peacefully at Manningtree, after a long sickness of a consumption, as many of his generation had done before him, without any trouble of conscience for what he had done, as was falsely reported of him.'[87] An entry in the Mistley parish register also confirms this, stating: 'Matthew Hopkins, son of Mr James Hopkins Minister of Wenham was buried at Mistley, August 12 1647', again confirming the end of one of the most controversial and reviled men in England's history.[88]

Chapter 5

Final Victims:
The Bideford Witches – 1682

Now listen to my Song, good People all,
And I shall tell what lately did befall.
At Exeter a place in Devonshire,
The like whereof of late you nere did hear.

At the last Assizes held in Exeter,
Three aged Women that imprisoned were
For Witches, and that many had destroy'd;
Were thither brought in order to be try'd.

Witchcraft Discovered and Punished[1]

As the seventeenth century drew to a close, prosecutions for witchcraft had been on the wane in England for some time, the ferocity of earlier decades giving way to a steady decline in both official accusations and executions for this once most feared of crimes. It wasn't that people didn't believe in witches anymore – far from it – but in the wake of the excesses of the Civil War period, official and learned discourse on witchcraft had moved on, and it was rare indeed to find either judge or jury willing to condemn those accused by their neighbours.

It was this very decline and shift away from prosecution that makes what took place in 1682 in the Devon town of Bideford all the more remarkable. Three women – Temperance Lloyd, Susannah Edwards and Mary Trembles – were accused of witchcraft. Not only that, but they were, shockingly for the times, found guilty of the charges against them and hanged.

According to the surviving sources, tensions had been brewing in the town for some time. Matters came to a head on 1 July 1682, when the elderly and widowed Temperance Lloyd was arrested by constables at the behest of local man Thomas Eastchurch. His grounds were clear: he suspected Temperance of causing illness and suffering to Grace Thomas, his sister-in-law, through witchcraft.

As Grace was to tell the town Mayor and two Justices two days later, in early February of 1681 she had suddenly begun to suffer from terrible pains in her head, arms and legs. The strange condition was not short-lived; she had been tormented by the pains until early August of that year. At that point the pains lessened somewhat and she was once again able to leave the house to walk and take the air, although at night she still suffered greatly.

It was during one of Grace's walks about the town that she had a strange encounter with Temperance Lloyd. On 30 September 1681, as she was walking up High Street, Temperance approached her in great agitation. Bursting into tears, Temperance fell to her knees, and expressed how pleased she was to see Grace well again. Perplexed, Grace asked why she was crying; the old woman responded that it was because she was so very glad to see Grace recovered from her illness.

That night, Grace had been taken ill again with excruciating pricking pains all over her body, from the top of her head right down to her feet. Her condition had not improved; the only slight consolation being that the pains were not *quite* so bad during the day as compared with at night.

She had continued in that sorry state until 1 July 1682, when matters worsened further; all of the pains concentrated in Grace's belly, which swelled to twice its normal size, so terrifying and painful that she had called out, thinking she would die. Indeed, she *had* appeared to be dead to those who witnessed the terrible scene, a state that lasted for the space of two hours. Although Grace recovered her senses, she spent the next month suffering from constant pricking pains in her heart, head, arms and legs – all over her body in fact, with no respite. It felt, Grace declared, as if she was being pinched, almost as if someone was trying to pull her flesh clean off her bones. Not only that, but she had been pulled from her bed by this unseen and powerful force, powerless to do anything to protect herself.

Suddenly, things had changed. On 1 July 1682, the day that Temperance Lloyd was arrested and taken to prison, Grace had immediately found relief, and although she still felt weak, she was no longer tormented by the terrible pains that had racked her body. There was only one explanation: Temperance was to blame for her illness.

The same day that Grace spoke to the Mayor and Justices, Elizabeth Eastchurch, wife of Thomas Eastchurch and sister to Grace, also gave evidence that corroborated her sister's story. As well as describing the same terrible illness that Grace had related, she added also how her sister had complained just the day before of a pricking feeling in her knee. When Elizabeth had examined the area, she had discovered nine marks, each like the prick of a thorn. Suspicions raised, Elizabeth had gone to visit Temperance where she was being held, demanding to know whether the old woman had made an image of Grace out of wax or clay and if she had pricked this to cause her pain. Temperance had denied doing any such thing, but had, ominously, admitted owning a piece of leather that she had pricked nine times.

Temperance herself was also examined on 3 July 1682. The Mayor and Justices did not mince words, asking about her dealings with the Devil. Temperance responded that around 30 September the previous year she had met with him in the middle of the afternoon in Higher Gunstone Lane. He had been, said Temperance, in the form of a 'black man', but she had known instinctively that it was the Devil all the same. When he had tried to convince her to go to the Eastchurch house in order to torment Grace Thomas, she had initially refused; it was only after a great deal of convincing that she had consented to go with him. Once at the Eastchurch house, Temperance had followed the man upstairs, where they both entered Grace's room. Anne Wakely, another Bideford resident, was there, rubbing and soothing Grace's arms in an attempt to help her pains. Temperance had started to pinch Grace Thomas on her shoulders, legs and arms, persisting for some time before she and the Devil finally left the poor woman alone. Upon reaching the street once more, Temperance recalled seeing a cat go into the Eastchurch shop, something considered of great significance.

When asked if she had returned to the Eastchurch house, Temperance said that she had done so; being invisible she had met with the cat she had seen previously. She had also returned there on another occasion with the Devil in his form as a man, the last time being 30 June. When they arrived Grace had been in a most sorry condition, but that did not stop the pair from pinching and pulling at her as before, almost pulling Grace out of her bed in the process. They had, Temperance admitted, been trying to kill her. She had not feared discovery, as the 'black man' had assured her that no one would discover her there or know what she had done. The Devil had also sucked at teats concealed on her body and she had knelt in the street for him to be able to do so, the black man being only the length of her arm. He had also sucked her on other occasions as she lay down, causing her a great deal of pain.

Given the nature of her confessions, the Mayor and the two Justices who listened to her account had further questions to ask of Temperance. This was not, it turned out, the first time her name had been linked to allegations of witchcraft. In 1670, she had been 'accused, indicted and arraigned, for practising of witchcraft upon the body of one William Herbert, late of Bideford, Husbandman'.[2] Temperance had been acquitted, but now she confessed that she had indeed been guilty of the crime, and that the Devil had convinced her to prick William Herbert to death. Furthermore, around 15 May 1679, she had been accused of witchcraft again, this time against Anne Fellow, the daughter of Edward and Anne Fellow, also of Bideford. At that time she had, Temperance recalled, been searched for marks and teats, but as they were not as obvious when she was younger, they had not been discovered. Accordingly, the matter had been dropped, but now Temperance confessed once again that she had been guilty, and was responsible for Anne Fellow's death.

Thomas Eastchurch also gave information on 3 July.[3] He recounted how, on 2 July, he had heard Temperance confess that on 30 September the previous year she had met 'something' in the form of a black man in Higher Gunstone Lane when she had been returning from the bakehouse. It was this man who had convinced her to go to the Eastchurch house in order to torment Grace Thomas. Temperance had told how she protested that Grace had done nothing to warrant such abuse, but that she allowed herself to be convinced to go and pinch and poke the other woman. Thomas Eastchurch added further that he believed initially that his sister-in-law was suffering from a 'distemper arising from a natural cause', and therefore she had visited several physicians; they had been unable to help her and had not brought relief for her symptoms or identified what had caused them.[4]

Anne Wakely, wife of William Wakely, was another Bideford resident to give her version of events. She had been attending Grace Thomas for the last six weeks of her illness, attempting to bring the suffering woman some relief from her pains. The day before, on 2 July, she had, on the order of the Mayor, searched Temperance Lloyd; Honor Hooper, one of the Eastchurches' servants, and other women were also present. In her search, Anne had discovered two teats in Temperance's private parts; each about an inch long, they looked as if they had been sucked by a child. When Anne had asked Temperance if this was where the 'black man' had sucked at her, Temperance told her that he had sucked her there many times, the last of which was 30 June. Anne also added that last Thursday, she had seen 'something' in the shape of a magpie at Grace Thomas's bedroom window, and that this had roused her suspicions. She had therefore questioned Temperance about it and the old woman had told her that it was not a bird at all, but the Devil, who had chosen to take that shape. Temperance also admitted that at the same time as the bird's appearance, she herself had in fact been downstairs, standing by the front door of the Eastchurch house. Anne's words were corroborated by Honor Hooper who also gave evidence that day.

Despite having given their version of events before the Mayor and Justices on 3 July, that was not enough for Thomas and Elizabeth Eastchurch. The piece of leather that Temperance had confessed to possessing and pricking still played on their minds, and the following day, with permission from the Mayor himself, Temperance was taken to St Mary's, Bideford's parish church.[5]

It is not recorded whether Temperance went willingly or not, although she would not have had much choice in the matter given that the move had the backing of those in authority in the town. In the church, she was questioned in the presence of Michael Ogilby, the Rector of Bideford, regarding her dealings with the Devil. When asked how long ago it was that the Devil had first 'tempted' her to evil ways, Temperance admitted that it was twelve years ago, when the Devil had convinced her to help kill William Herbert in exchange for the promise that all would be well with her from then on. She also confessed to having caused the death of Anne Fellow. Where Grace Thomas was concerned, she admitted that on 23 June she had gone into the Eastchurch shop in the form of a cat. Whilst there, she had taken a 'puppet or picture' to Grace Thomas's room, and left it somewhere near the woman's bed; Temperance denied that she had stuck pins into this item, despite the pressing of those who questioned her. When asked to reveal the location of the puppet she had left in Grace Thomas's room in the Eastchurch house, Temperance again refused to cooperate, citing the belief that the Devil would 'tear her in pieces' if she revealed the hiding place.[6]

There was some victory for her interrogators; the old woman now confessed to the death of Jane Dallyn, wife of a Bideford Mariner named Simon Dallyn. This latter mischief she had carried out by secretly pricking Jane in the eye, a fact that had never been discovered before now. Also added to the growing list of those Temperance had harmed through witchcraft was Lydia Burman, a woman who had testified against her at the trial regarding the murder of William Herbert and who was now, ominously it seemed, dead.[7]

It is unclear how long Temperance underwent such questioning or whether the Eastchurch couple were satisfied with what they had heard. Temperance was further pressed by the rector to recite the Lord's Prayer and the Creed but was, unfortunately for her, unable to do so without mistakes, despite several attempts at each.

Temperance was returned to the lockup in the old chapel, situated towards the west end of the bridge at Bideford.[8] It is to be expected that, given the conditions of prisons and lockups of the time, it would not have been a pleasant experience during her stay there. Worse was to come; on 8 July, she was transferred to Exeter, where she was held at Rougemont Castle to await her fate.

Probably unbeknownst to Temperance, two other local women were now to enter the story. On Monday 17 July, blacksmith William Edwards overheard the widowed Susannah Edwards make a startling confession. He had, he claimed, heard her confess that she had slept with the Devil, and also that he had sucked her breast and the teat in her 'secret parts'.[9] He had also heard Susannah confess that she and another woman, Mary Trembles, had gone invisible to the house of John Barnes with the purpose of killing his wife Grace. On the strength of this, the following day Susannah Edwards was apprehended, along with Mary, her supposed accomplice.[10]

As with Temperance Lloyd, several people came forward to give their evidence against the two women. On 18 July Joan, the wife of Anthony Jones, told how on that very day she had been with Susannah Edwards, when John Dunning of Great Torrington came to visit her. In Joan's hearing, Dunning had demanded to know of Susannah how she had become a witch. Susannah had told him that although she had refused to confess to it before that point, now she would confess to him. She had gone on to tell Dunning that one day she had been out gathering wood when a gentleman approached her. Hoping to gain some charity from him, she had curtsied and listened to what he had to say. This meeting had taken place in Parsonage Close. Furthermore, once Dunning had left, Joan heard Susannah and Mary confess that on Sunday 16 July they had pricked Grace Barnes together, along with the help of the Devil. This was not the only time she had done so either; they had pricked Grace again that very day. Joan Jones had then witnessed something of an altercation between Susannah Edwards and Mary Trembles. According to Joan, Mary had told Susannah: 'O thou rogue, I will now confess all: for 'tis thou that hast made me to be a witch, and thou are one thy self, and my conscience must swear it.'

Susannah had replied: 'I did not think that thou wouldst have been such a rogue to discover it.' Furthermore, Susannah had confessed that the Devil 'did oftentimes carry about her spirit.'[11] She also confessed to tormenting Dorcas Coleman, and that the Devil, in the shape of a boy, had lain with her and sucked at her before having carnal knowledge of her several times.

Unlike with Temperance, Susannah's mischief did not end with her apprehension. Joan's husband Anthony had grown suspicious whilst watching Susannah, the old woman busy twisting and fiddling with her hands against herself. 'Thou Devil,' he had exclaimed, 'thou art now tormenting some person or other.'[12] Rather than denying the matter, Susannah had ominously retorted, 'Well enough, I will fit thee.'[13]

Whilst all of this was occurring, Grace Barnes had continued to suffer. To provide further evidence against Susannah, Anthony Jones and one of the constables had been sent by the mayor to bring the suffering woman to the Town Hall. When they returned with the sick woman, Susannah had turned about and looked at Anthony Jones as he approached. Immediately he had been taken ill, declaring, 'Wife, I am now bewitched by this Devil!'[14] He had then proceeded to leap and caper alarmingly, 'and fell a shaking, quivering, and foaming' lying on the ground for half an hour as if dying or dead.[15] When he had finally come round, said Joan, her husband had told her and others that Susannah had bewitched him. She had never known her husband to suffer like that before, and he was usually well in both body and mind.

Susannah herself was also examined before the Mayor and Justices regarding her supposed witchcraft against Grace Barnes. It had started, Susannah told them, when she had met a gentleman in Parsonage Close; dressed all in black he had cut a fine figure, and, hoping to beg some money from him, she had curtsied politely. When asked whether she was a poor woman, she had answered in the affirmative, and the man promised that if she did one thing for him she would never want again for anything. Suitably overwhelmed, Susannah had exclaimed 'In the name of God, what is it I should have?' only for the gentleman to vanish. When asked who this gentleman was, Susannah revealed to her questioners that he was none other than the Devil.

Not long after that first encounter, a boy, or rather something in the shape of one, came to her house. Susannah was not fooled, and she was certain that this was the Devil again, come to her in another form. Despite this, she had allowed the boy to lie with her and suck at her breast.

Furthermore, she had met with him again, in Stambridge Lane; when he sucked her breast that time, he had drawn blood.

With her relationship with the Devil well established, Susannah went on to admit how, on Sunday 16 July, she and Mary Trembles had gone to the Barnes household unseen, and pricked and pinched Grace Barnes terribly until she was almost dead. Her reason was that the Devil had told her to, and he had also promised that he would come to her again, once more before she would leave the town.[16]

Susannah confessed also that she could go anywhere she liked due to being able to turn herself invisible. Not only that, it would appear that she was still lying in her bed to others who saw her there. Asked if she had hurt anyone other than Grace Barnes, Susannah replied in the affirmative; she had caused suffering to another woman: Dorcas Coleman.

Mary Trembles too was examined. Accused likewise of bewitching Grace Barnes, she was asked how long she had been practising witchcraft. Mary recounted how, three years earlier, Susannah Edwards had told her that if she did as Susannah told her, then she would not be in want when it came to money, meat, drink or clothes. After that, the Devil had come to her in the shape of a lion and lay with her in that form, and he had also sucked her in her private parts, so hard that it made her cry out in pain.

Following this, Mary had been out begging for bread and meat when she had met Susannah, who asked where she had been. When she told her, Susannah had said that they would go together to John Barnes's house to ask for bread and meat there. When they got to the Barnes' residence, John Barnes was absent and his wife Grace and her servant refused to give the women what they wanted. Not to be put off, later that day Susannah had told Mary to return to the Barnes' house, this time to ask for some tobacco. Despite her optimism, this attempt was as unsuccessful as the first, and Mary returned to Susannah to tell her so. Displeased at the refusal, Susannah remarked that it would have been better for Grace to have given Mary what she had asked for.

On 16 July, she and Susannah had gone to John Barnes's house again. This time they had been invisible and had easily managed to get inside. Finding the room where Grace lay in bed with her husband, they had then pricked and pinched her nearly to death.

When asked how many times the Devil had known her carnally besides the time mentioned, Mary said that there had been three other times, the last being 16 July when she was on her way to the bakehouse. On that occasion she would, Mary insisted, have gone on to kill Grace Barnes, and had only been prevented from doing so when she had spilt some of the meat she was carrying.

John Barnes also spoke of his wife's suffering. On 18 May, Grace had suddenly experienced sharp pricking pains in her arms, stomach and breast, the pain being so strong that it felt as if she were being 'stabbed with awls'.[17] She had been in such great pain that he had been convinced she would die from it then and there. His wife had survived, but the pains continued to varying degrees, and she still suffered from them two months on. Two days earlier on 16 July, Grace's pains had grown stronger again, and it had taken four men and women to hold her down as she struggled in agony. During the commotion, Agnes Whitefield heard someone at the door and had found Mary Trembles standing there. Mary, a single woman, had a white pot in her hands, looking for all the world as if she were going to the local bakehouse. When Grace was told who had been at the door, the suffering woman had exclaimed that Mary was one of the very people to blame for her condition, and that she had now come to finish the job by killing her.

On 19 July, Anthony Jones was apparently recovered enough from his fit to corroborate his wife's testimony against Susannah Edwards. He too recounted how the day before he had seen Susannah 'gripe and twinkle her hands upon her own body, in an unusual manner'.[18] When he had accused her of tormenting someone, she threatened to 'fit' him, and, when he returned to the Town Hall with Grace Barnes, he was taken ill and had called out to his wife: 'Wife, I am now bewitched by this Devil, Susannah Edwards.'[19]

On the strength of the damning information given against them and their own confessions, Susannah and Mary were taken to gaol in Exeter on 19 July. With all three women imprisoned, on 26 July 1682, Dorcas Coleman was also well enough to give her evidence against Susannah. Towards the end of August 1680 she had fallen seriously ill, plagued by 'tormenting pains, by pricking in her arms, stomach and heart'. She had never felt anything like it before, and had sent Thomas Bremincom, her husband's uncle, to Doctor George Beare for help. He had come in good haste, but had told her that there was nothing he could do to lessen her pains, as their cause was not merely physical – she had been bewitched. There was no question as to who was behind the bewitching; Dorcas had seen the spectral form of Susannah Edwards in her room.

When Susannah Edwards had been arrested for causing harm to Grace Barnes, Dorcas Coleman had taken the opportunity to visit her in prison. Susannah had there confessed to her and admitted to likewise being the cause of Dorcas's illness, falling to her knees to beg for forgiveness and to ask Dorcas to pray for her.

Thomas Bremincom gave evidence on the same day, corroborating Dorcas Coleman's version of events from two years previously. He too had seen Susannah Edwards in the room, and although Dorcas had tried to get up to attack her, the woman was not able to get herself out of the chair. He and John Coleman tried to help Dorcas up, but were unable to do so successfully with Susannah still in the room. When Susannah was finally almost out of the room, Dorcas had slid from her chair trying, on her back, to follow the other woman out of the room. Again, the two men tried to help her, but were unable to do so until Susannah Edwards had gone down the stairs. When in the worst of her suffering, Dorcas was unable to speak, but could point in the direction in which Susannah Edwards had left; on going to the door to check, it was ascertained that – although unable to see the other woman – Dorcas had been correct.

As July turned to August 1682, Grace Barnes gave her version of events. She had experienced great pains in her body for several years, and even though she had sought to be cured wherever possible, it was only a year-and-a-half ago that she had thought witchcraft might be behind her suffering, and only then when some physicians had suggested this cause. She now suspected Susannah Edwards of being responsible for her condition because she often came to their house for either very trivial matters or for no given reason at all. In May of 1682 she had experienced a very bad attack, with terrible pricking pains in her arms, breast and heart which lasted several days and nights. Grace accused Susannah Edwards and also Mary Trembles of being responsible for her pains.

Finally, on 12 August, William Herbert, blacksmith and the son of the man Temperance had now admitted to killing through witchcraft, also gave evidence. In February 1670, his father had told him on his deathbed that Temperance Lloyd had bewitched him and that she was the cause of his imminent death. Herbert had also told his son that after his death, his family should check his body, because they would be sure to find proof of the witchcraft done to him, and requested that Temperance be arrested for his murder.[20] William had not forgotten the matter, and on 4 July 1682, had visited Temperance in prison and demanded of her whether she had caused harm to his father. Temperance had not equivocated, admitting, 'Surely William I did kill thy father.'[21] William asked whether she had likewise been responsible for Lydia Burman's condition, Temperance replied that yes, she had killed her also. When asked why she had not confessed during her first arrest in 1671, Temperance responded with the cryptic response that her time had not been over then and that the Devil had given her great power and more time to use it in. William also said that he had heard Temperance admit to the deaths of Anne Fellow and Jane Dallyn.

At the Assizes in Exeter on 14 August, despite pleading not guilty, all three women were found guilty of the indictments against them: Temperance for witchcraft on the body of Grace Thomas, Mary Trembles for witchcraft against Grace Barnes, and Susannah for the same against Dorcas Coleman. All three were sentenced to death.[22] Interestingly, Temperance was cleared of the charge of Lydia Burman's death and found not guilty.

On 25 August the condemned women were taken to the gallows at Heavitree, just outside Exeter, but their ordeals were not over yet. Before they were executed, each woman was questioned in turn by a man named Mr Hann, and asked to confess again to the crimes they were to die for.

Mary Trembles was first and, despite her previous confessions, now denied that the Devil had known her carnally, sucked at her, or that she had teats in her private parts. Indeed, she had only met the Devil on one occasion; she had cried out and he had vanished and had given her nothing. Even when pressed to confess further, Mary refused, stating she had already said everything she would on the matter.

Temperance, despite having confessed to several things during her time in prison, when questioned at the gallows it was another matter. She too denied having made a contract with the Devil or allowing him to suck her blood. Neither had he known her carnally. When asked what he did with her, Temperance still maintained that she had harmed Grace Thomas, but insisted now that she was the only victim of her malice. She also refused to admit to causing damage to ships or boats by overturning them, or causing harm to any mariners in her acquaintance when asked to do so.[23]

Susannah Edwards was the last to face questioning amidst the loudness of the crowd that had come to see their end. She too denied everything set before her. The denials of the three women did them no good, a fact they must have known as they faced their last minutes of life. Released from questioning, the condemned took part in prayers that were said for their souls, and at Susannah's request, part of psalm 40 was sung.

As the women were executed in turn, their final words, or an idealised version of them, were recorded for posterity. According to the record, Susannah met her end first, uttering the words: 'The Lord Jesus speed [*sic*] me though my sins be as red as scarlet, the Lord Jesus can make them as white as snow. The Lord help my soul.'[24] Mary Trembles was next, praying 'Lord Jesus receive my soul, Lord Jesus speed me.'[25]

Temperance was last, requesting that 'Jesus Christ speed me well: Lord forgive all my sins; Lord Jesus Christ be merciful to my poor soul.'[26] Even then she was not to be allowed to find peace, and was questioned further before being finally sent into oblivion, avowing that she believed in God and Jesus, and that she prayed for Jesus to forgive her sins.[27]

Thus the women who have come to be known as the Bideford Witches met their end that summer's day, bringing satisfactorily to a close what had been a most troubling affair for the people of the town, whilst creating one of the greatest injustices in England during the period of the witch trials.

****

The sources for the Bideford case are several and also, in some cases, contradictory. The year of the execution itself saw the production of two, possibly three, pamphlets relating the events that had taken place. The rather excessively titled:

> A true and impartial relation of the informations against three witches, viz, Temperance Lloyd, Mary Trembles, and Susannah Edwards, who were indicted, arraigned and convicted at the Assizes holden for the county of Devon at the Castle of Exon, Aug 14 1682. With their several confessions, taken before Thomas Gist Mayor and John Davi Alderman of Bideford in the said county, where they were inhabitants. As also their speeches, confessions and behaviour, at the time and place of execution on the twenty fifth of the said month.

is the longest of the three at forty-four pages long, and considered to be the most accurate as it is made up primarily of evidence and statements given by the various people who spoke against the accused women.

The second pamphlet is:

> The tryal, condemnation and execution of three witches, viz. Temperance Floyd, Mary Floyd, and Susannah Edwards. Who

were arraigned at Exeter on the 18th August 1682. And being proved guilty of witchcraft, were condemned to be hanged, which was accordingly executed in view of many spectators, whose strange and much to be lamented impudence, is never to be forgotten. Also, how they confessed what mischiefs they had done, by the assistance of the Devil, who lay with the above-named Temperance Floyd nine nights together. Also how they squeezed one Hannah Thomas to death in their arms; how they also caused several ships to be cast away, causing a boy to fall from the top of a main-mast into the sea. With many wonderful things, worth your reading.

Just from a glance through the various inaccuracies in the title alone it can be supposed that this account would be less likely to hold the truth than the first.[28] This source relates how Temperance did not seem to understand what lay before her and that she was 'unconcerned' and eating merrily all the way to the place of execution. It is this same source that relates how Mary, in quite the opposite fashion, was most uncooperative; she refused to go with the others when the time came, and had to be tied to a horse and forcibly dragged to Heavitree.[29] It has also been generally accepted, perhaps on the strength of this, that Temperance at least was not of sound mind, or at the very least somewhat 'simple', though there is no other evidence throughout the available sources to suggest or support this claim.

The life and conversation of Temperance Floyd, Mary Lloyd and Susannah Edwards three eminent witches, lately condemned at Exeter Assizes; together with a full account of their first agreement with the Devil; with the manner how they prosecuted their devilish sorceries. Also a full account of their trial, examination, condemnation and confession, at the place of execution: with many other things remarkable and worthy observation.

Is the third account.[30] This is the most fanciful of the three pamphlets and reveals such snippets as how Temperance had been slapped across the face by the Devil, leaving his mark there for all to see. Temperance was also claimed to be the 'most notorious' out of the three condemned, having tempted the other two into their wicked ways and frequently taking the Devil into her bed.[31]

As is often the problem with such cases, most of what we can learn about the women involved in the Bideford trial comes from the snapshots provided in the 'evidence' given by those accusing them, and their own recorded confessions. What can be interesting details about their lives in general are therefore often omitted as seen as not directly relevant to the accusations and cases being built up against them. There are, however, several things that we can learn regarding Temperance, Susannah and Mary that help place the women in their social and cultural context.

Susannah Edwards was born Susannah or Susan Winslade, the illegitimate or natural daughter of Rachel Winslade on 2 December 1612.[32] She was, therefore, 70 at the time of being accused. Susannah married David Edwards in 1639, but was widowed by the time she was accused of witchcraft, her husband having died in 1662. Although one commentator stresses the fact that the accused women were isolated, alone and childless, this was not true in Susannah's case, as she had at least five children during her marriage.[33]

Mary Trembles is recorded as a single woman and, as she was born in 1630 was 52 years of age at her trial.[34] Out of the three women involved in the Bideford case, it is of Mary that least is known, and there is no further biographical trace of her or her family in the parish registers.

The thing that is most often remarked upon regarding Temperance Lloyd is her age, and several of the sources on the trial refer to her as elderly and being around 70 years old. Although she was a widow there is no record of children born to her, nor of whom her husband might have been. He was already dead by the time Temperance was first accused of witchcraft in 1671. There is no record of her maiden name, and therefore attempts to trace her family before her marriage come to a standstill.[35] Temperance was clearly in Bideford from the 1670s, giving lie to the suggestion put forward that the accused women were newcomers to the area, and that this fact played a part in what happened to them.

Intriguingly, William Edwards, one of the people to speak out against Susannah and who overheard her confessing to bewitching Grace Barnes, was in fact likely a relation of the old woman by marriage. The Edwards family had been established in Bideford since at least the turn of the century, and David Edwards, Susannah's late husband, appears to have been one of at least three brothers, one of whom was called William. He and another brother in turn had sons of that name, and it is highly likely that it was one of these three Williams that made the initial accusation against either their sister-in-law or aunt.

What *is* known for certain of all three women is that they were suffering from the poverty that had struck many in Bideford in the closing quarter of the seventeenth century, and Temperance, Susannah and Mary were all listed as receiving poor relief. By their own admission and the testimony of others, Susannah Edwards and Mary Trembles were both known for begging from their neighbours.[36]

The town itself had developed into a bustling and well-off port, due largely to successful trade links with America, focusing on tobacco and the wool trade. Despite this, poverty was an increasing problem for the population of just over 2,500. Bideford was not alone in this predicament; the gap between the wealthy and the poor was rapidly widening in an increasing number of towns and cities throughout England.[37] To make matters worse, 1682 was, across the country, a time of general shortage and scarcity of food and resources; this would have further heightened tensions between those who were reduced to begging, such as Mary Trembles and Susannah Edwards, and those to whom they turned for help and who were either unwilling or, if their own conditions were straitened, unable, to give their usual assistance.[38]

Along with the economical strains within the town, the social, religious and political situation in Bideford at the time was fraught with tension. The non-conformist population was steadily growing; although there were only ninety-six official non-conformists recorded in Bideford in 1674, there were said to have been closer to 400 at one meeting that took place in that same year, causing great alarm for the authorities.[39] There is, however, no evidence to place any of the accused women in the non-conformist camp so this cannot be seen as a reason for their persecution and eventual fate. Likewise, the years leading up to the trial of the Bideford witches had seen a steady build up of tension, not helped by the fact that the key authority figures in the town – Thomas Gist, the Mayor, the town clerk John Hill, and Michael Ogilby the rector – were all contentious men to say the least. Instead of maintaining peace and order as would have been expected, these men were often at the very centre of pockets of discord, both between themselves and with those over whom they held authority. In turn, the people of the town displayed a marked lack of respect for their superiors, and disorder was rife.[40] This volatile environment could not have failed to play a crucial role in the events that took place, acting as a catalyst that at the very least enabled the accusations to take hold in the first place.

What must not be overlooked is that, initially at least, the matter was driven very much by Thomas Eastchurch and those of his household. The impetus for the Bideford affair was the accusation against Temperance made by Eastchurch, and it was his dissatisfaction over the matter of the pricked piece of leather that led to Temperance being brought to the church for further questioning. Those who gave evidence against her were all connected to the Eastchurch couple in some way: Wakely was attendant for Grace Thomas for the last six weeks of her being ill, and Honor Hooper was a servant of Thomas Eastchurch. It must also be remembered that Grace Thomas was the sister of Elizabeth Eastchurch. It might well have been the unrest in the town that spurred Eastchurch to act, but it cannot be argued that the initial pursuit of the women was politically motivated.

As for Susannah and Mary, they were not accused until after Temperance had been arrested, and there is no indication that the Eastchurch group bore the other two women any ill-will or were even aware of their existence. There is also very little evidence for Temperance being connected to the other two accused women in any way; the only time that they are linked in the original sources is at their execution: Temperance was intriguingly asked at the gallows whether it had been she or Susannah who had bewitched 'the children', and was also blamed for being 'the woman that has debauched the other two'.[41]

Although not named in the main account of the case, two other Bideford women were also accused of witchcraft in 1682: Elizabeth Caddy and Mary Beare.[42] It has been stated that there is no further information known about either woman save for their names and the outcome of the charges against them; however, a dig through the parish registers for Bideford provides some previously overlooked biographical information that is of interest. An Elizabeth Caddy or Caddie, daughter of Richard Caddy, was born in 1653, putting her at just shy of 30 years old when Temperance Lloyd was accused. Very little is known about Elizabeth, but she was accused by Mary Weekes on Friday 21 July 1582; released on bail, she was later indicted and appeared before the same Assizes as the three who were executed, but the charges were thrown out by the grand jury.[43]

Mary Beare, the other woman accused, was the daughter of Roger and Grace Beare; born in 1608, she was 74 years old at the time of being accused, and potentially the oldest of the five Bideford women associated with witchcraft that year.[44] Mary was not prosecuted and did not make it as far as the assizes, and the accusations against her or who they were made by are therefore unknown.

It is unclear whether Elizabeth and Mary knew of, or were known to, the three less fortunate Bideford women who were accused of witchcraft in 1682, and as no mention is made of them in the pamphlet accounts of the case the only light to be shed on the matter is what we can learn from the sessions book. Gent suggests that Caddy and Beare were of higher standing socially than the other three and that this played a hand in matters not being pursued further against them.[45] It is also entirely possible that there was simply not enough evidence to bring a case to bear against Elizabeth Caddy and Mary Beare; that, coupled with either a lack of standing or vociferousness from their accusers, may have been what made all the difference between them going to the noose and walking free.[46]

One question that continues to puzzle those interested in the case is why the three women confessed to anything in the first place, spawning numerous theories that are applicable to witchcraft confessions in general and also specific to the Bideford case itself.

The idea of the accused deciding – either consciously or subconsciously – on a path of suicide was one of the earliest motivations ascribed to the condemned women.[47] Although a tempting and tidy solution, and one that is potentially valid in other instances of confession, in this case it does not account for the women retracting their confessions at the gallows, unless one argues for a sudden change of heart on the part of all three, and therefore this theory cannot wholly account for the words of Temperance and her fellow accused.

Another theory is linked to the idea that those questioning the women at different times used leading language and questions which in turn produced the answers they wanted and expected. This would mean that the confessions made by Temperance, Susannah and Mary reflected more about what their questioners wanted to hear than what the women themselves believed had occurred. It has been pointed out that the more outlandish elements of the three women's confessions reflected opinions and ideas of witchcraft held by the educated and elite classes, those who had read and discussed, and ultimately been influenced by, the literature of the day on witchcraft and demonism. By contrast, the things the women confessed to when they were first apprehended and questioned were more in line with popular beliefs regarding witchcraft and the harm that could be done by those maliciously motivated to use it, illustrating again the divide between learned and popular ideas of witchcraft, what it meant to be a witch, and, most importantly, which of the two would ultimately prevail.

Although the accused women were not connected in a typical sense, where parallels can be drawn is between the similarities in the symptoms and illnesses described by the supposed victims of the three 'witches'. Most notably, the main witnesses who spoke out against Temperance, Susannah and Mary described sharp pricking pains to various parts of their bodies, and in all cases their suffering spanned a long period of time. Such descriptions will be familiar to anyone with a working knowledge of witchcraft accusations and it is interesting to observe how the Bideford sufferers fit into a pre-existing narrative and understanding of such conditions. There has been speculation that Grace Thomas was actually sick, and that her death a couple of years later in 1686 suggests that she was suffering from a long-term illness that finally claimed her life.[48] Grace Barnes seems to have lived until 1713, although there is no account of whether or not she continued to suffer after the 'witches' were executed. Although Susannah and Mary were officially accused after Temperance, Dorcas Coleman was actually taken ill *before* Grace Thomas, and it is interesting to note that Dorcas, as has already been seen, was no stranger to the details of witchcraft accusations and the symptoms involved therein. Whether her role in matters has been understated or not is impossible to confirm, it is at least possible that her memory of the evidence given against Temperance previously along with Lydia Burman's death from suspected witchcraft played a part in Dorcas's own interpretation of a natural illness.[49]

There is of course the possibility that the women believed what they said, and that the things they did admit to and spoke of were true, whilst those they did not were created by those who questioned them. This again does not quite ring true; although Temperance was steadfast in her insistence that she was guilty of harming Grace until her last moments, going to her death adamant that she had tormented her victim at the behest of the Devil, both Susannah and Mary took back everything they had previously confessed, suggesting therefore a less-than-firm belief in their own pronouncements.

One popular and persuasive idea is that the three women were executed ultimately for the perceived greater good, the fear of increased social unrest and potential uprising if they were declared innocent outweighing the necessity of establishing the truth.[50] The idea that the women were scapegoats of sorts, and that they were executed in order to avoid the town descending into a witch-hunting frenzy was not without precedent: Elizabeth Peacock was acquitted by jury in 1670 and 1672, but was gaoled regardless on the complaint of a man who feared for the devaluation of his estate if she went free. Likewise, Anne Rawlins was sent to the local House of Correction despite being acquitted, on the opinion of those higher up the social scale than herself. The chilling idea that those conducting the trial were well aware that the accused were likely innocent but saw them go to the gallows anyway is one that cannot, given the evidence, be discounted.

The injustice carried out against the three women from Bideford has not gone un-remarked in recent years. In 2013 a plaque commemorating the tragedy was put up at Rougemont Castle, Exeter, where they met their fate, with the moving and hopeful words:

> The Devon Witches
> In Memory Of
> Temperance Lloyd
> Susannah Edwards
> Mary Trembles
> Of Bideford Died 1682
> Alice Molland
> Died 1685
> The Last People in England To Be Executed For Witchcraft
> Tried Here And Hanged At Heavitree
> In the hope of an end to persecution and intolerance.

Despite the wording of the memorial, there has been much debate regarding whether the Bideford Witches or Alice Molland do indeed hold the non-honour of being the last to be executed for witchcraft in England. Alice Molland was tried by Sir Francis North and Sir Thomas Raymond – the justices who oversaw the trial of the Bideford Witches – at the Exeter Lent Assizes in 1684 on the charge of witchcraft on the body of Jane or Joane and Wilmot Snow and Agnes Furze. She was found guilty and sentenced to hang, but as there is no official record of her execution, it is impossible to verify for certain that she did suffer the same fate as Temperance, Mary and Susannah, or whether she escaped the noose.[51] Across the country, from the Home Circuit and Middlesex Sessions the last recorded execution took place in 1660, and there hadn't been an execution for witchcraft on the Western Circuit, of which Exeter was a part, since 1671.[52] This final spate in the 1680s therefore were something of an anomaly, and this again highlights the peculiar conditions of the Bideford trial.[53]

Unsurprisingly, the case of the execution of the three women from Bideford has attracted much interest over the years. Local legend has it that the three witches who were condemned had lived together in a cottage in Upper Gunstone; although it burned down in the late nineteenth century, the story of the three women sharing an abode lives on in popular imagination, proving once again the tenacious hold such tales can have. The sorry tale of their accusation and execution has been recounted, with varying degrees of accuracy, in various books, and has also been dramatised on several occasions.[54]

In Exeter itself, a recent mural can be seen in Musgrave Row showing various events from the history of the city; the Bideford Witches are included in the scene, highlighting, whether for good or not, they have not been forgotten.[55] A petition was also launched in 2013 in a bid to gain the women pardon, with the following wording:

> We ask HM Government to Pardon Temperance Lloyd, Susannah Edwards and Mary Trembles of Bideford for the crime of Witchcraft.
>
> They were hanged on August 25th 1682 at Heavitree, Exeter, convicted for actions they could not have committed, under a law that no longer exists.
> They were convicted on hearsay evidence under the 1604 Statute against Witchcraft devised under King James I – who believed his cousin had tried to assassinate him by raising a storm at sea using witchcraft.
> Leading theologians abetted their conviction by defining the 'Attributes of Witches' and by declaring 'to deny witchcraft is to deny God'.
> The assizes Justices did not believe them guilty but responded to an angry mob that called for a hanging.
>
> Pardoning the 'Bideford Witches' would acknowledge their innocence and that of over 450 others executed in the name of good government.[56]

Although backed by a local MP, the petition received less than 500 signatures and there was some controversy over whether the women should be pardoned or whether it was more important to keep the memory of the injustice alive. The petition has since been archived, but its very creation highlights the enduring memory of the witch trials across England and the crucial place they hold in the history of a people who, ever more so today, are dangerously divided.

Afterword

History is, by necessity, told by the winners. In the case of England's witch trials, this meant those who made and then upheld the accusations that brought so many to the gallows, usually those with money and influence behind the pen that recorded the outcome for generations to come. Despite this, the words of the victims, the accused, the persecuted, cannot be fully stifled; their personalities and ordeals seeping through in spite, or perhaps because, of the way they were treated by those who sought to silence them. It is through these often fleeting glimpses that their names are remembered, their words and actions recorded, and their stories, ultimately, never forgotten.

I hope this book goes some way towards continuing their legacy: the reminder that we should never lose sight of what humankind has been capable of, and what, if we are not careful, might be capable of again.

Willow Winsham, October, 2017.

Select Bibliography

Mistley Parish Registers, 1647, Burial Record for Matthew Hopkins D/P 343/1/1
John Andrew's Trust Account Book entries for 1679 NDRO B1003/1/1
John Andrew's Trust Account Book entries for 1680 and 1681 NDRO B1003/1/1
Bideford Quarter Sessions Records, 1682 NDRO 1064Q-SQ-1

Almond, Philip C, *The Witches of Warboys*, I.B Tauris, 2008.
A True and Impartial Relation of the Informations Against Three Witches, London, 1682
A true and just Record, of the Information, Examination and Confession of all the Witches, taken at S. Oses [sic] in the county of Essex: whereof some were executed, and other some entreated according to the determination of law.
Anon, *A Magazine of Scandall. Or, A Heap of wickedness of two infamous Ministers*, London, 1642.
Anonymous, *The Lawes against Witches and Conjuration and Some brief Notes and Observations for the Discovery of Witches*, London, 1645.
The Moderate Intelligencer, 4–11 Sept, 1645.
The life and conversation of Temperance Floyd, Mary Lloyd and Susannah Edwards three eminent witches, lately condemned at Exeter Assizes; 1682.
The tryal, condemnation and execution of three witches, viz. Temperance Floyd, Mary Floyd, and Susannah Edwards. 1682.
Barger, George, *Ergot and Ergotism*, London, Gurney and Jackson 1931.
Barry, Jonathan, *Witchcraft and Demonism in South West England*, (Palgrave Historical Studies in Witchcraft and Magic) AIAA, 2012.
Bennett, Walter, *The Pendle Witches*, Lancashire Country Council 1976.
Benard, Richard, A Guide to Grand-Jury Men, London 1627.
Briggs, Robin, *Witches and Neighbours*, New York, Penguin 1996.
Brown, Peter, *Essex Witches*, The History Press 2014.
Cabell, Craig, *Witchfinder General: The Biography of Matthew Hopkins*, Stroud, The History Press 2006.
Cockburn, J. S., (ed), *Calendar of Assize Records: Essex Indictments Elizabeth I*, London, Stationary Office 1978.
Cotta, John, *A Short Discoverie of the Unobserved Dangers*, London, 1612.

SELECT BIBLIOGRAPHY

Crawford, Patricia, Mendelson Sara, *Women in Early Modern England,* Oxford, Clarendon 1998.

Davies, Owen, *Witchcraft, Magic and Culture 1736–1951,* Manchester University Press 1999.

Davies, Owen, *Popular Magic: Cunning Folk in English History,* London, Continuum 2007.

Davies, R. T., *Four Centuries of Witch Beliefs,* London, Routledge 2011.

Deacon, Richard, *Matthew Hopkins Witch Finder General,* London, Anchor Press 1976.

Gordon, Dee, Infamous Essex Women,

Ehrenreich, Barbara and Deirdre English, *Witches, Midwives, and Nurses: A History of Women Healers, Contemporary Classics by Women,* Feminist Press, 2010.

Ellis, Sir Henry, *The Visitation of the County of Huntingdon, 1849, Camden Society, London*

Ewen, C. L'Estrange, (ed.) *Witch Hunting and Witch Trials,* London, Kegan Paul, Trench, Trubner & Co. 1929.

Ewen, C. L'Estrange, (ed.) *Witchcraft and Demonism,* London, Heath Cranton 1933.

Fletcher, Anthony, *Gender, Sex and Subordination in England, 1500–1800,* Newhaven and London, Yale 1999.

Gaskill, Malcolm, *Witchfinders: A Seventeenth-Century English Tragedy,* London, John Murray Publishers 2006.

Gaskill, Malcolm, *Witchcraft: A Very Short Introduction,* Oxford, Oxford University Press 2010.

Gent, Frank J., *The Trial of the Bideford Witches*, Crediton, 2001.

Gibson, Marion, *Early Modern Witches: Witchcraft Cases in Contemporary Writing,* London, Routledge, 2000.

Gibson, Marion, (ed.) *Witchcraft and Society in England and America, 1550–1750,* New York, Cornell University Press 2003.

Harley, David, 'Historians as Demonologists: The Myth of the Midwife-Witch' Social History of Medicine Volume 3, Issue 1.

Hopkins, Matthew, *The Discovery of Witches*, London, 1646.

Hutchinson, Francis, *An Historical Essay Concerning Witchcraft,* London 1718.

Inderwick, F. A,. *Side-Lights on the Stuarts*, London, 1888.

James I, *Daemonologie*: London, 1603.

Laurence, Anne, *Women in England 1500–1760,* London, Phoenix Press 2002.

Lumby, Jonathan, *The Lancashire Witch-Craze: Jennet Preston and the Lancashire Witches, 1612,* Preston, Carnegie, 1995.

Macfarlane, Alan, *Witchcraft in Tudor and Stuart England, London,* Routledge 1999.

Maxwell-Stuart, P. G., *Witch Hunters,* Stroud, Tempus 2003.

Maxwell-Stuart, P. G., *The British Witch: The Biography,* Stroud, Amberley 2014.

Murray, Margaret Alice, *The Witch-Cult in Western Europe*, Oxford, Clarendon 1921.

Notestein, Wallace, *A History of Witchcraft in England from 1558–1718,* Baltimore, Lord Baltimore Press, 1911.

Poole, Robert, (ed.) *The Lancashire Witches: Histories and Stories*, Manchester, Manchester University Press, 2002.

Report and Transactions of the Devonshire Association, Vol 47, Devonshire Association, 1915.

Rosen, Barbara, *Witchcraft in England, 1558–1618*, University of Massachusetts Press, Amhurst, 1991.

Serpell, James A., *Guardian Spirits or Demonic Pets: The Concept of the Witch's Familiar in Early Modern England, 1530–1712: The Animal/Human Boundary*, Rochester, NY: Rochester University Press 2002.

Stearne, John, *A Confirmation and Discovery of Witchcraft*, 1648.

Stone, Lawrence, *Uncertain Unions and Broken Lives,* Oxford, Oxford University Press 1995.

Thomas, Keith, *Religion and the Decline of Magic,* London, Penguin, 1991.

Whittaker, Gladys, *Roughlee Hall: Fact and Fiction*, Marsden Antiquarians, 1980.

Notes

Chapter 1

1. Agnes Waterhouse, an elderly widow from Hatfield Peverel, went to the gallows on 29 July 1566 for bewitching local man William Fynee to death. Shortly after her accession to the English throne, Elizabeth I passed the 1563 Witchcraft Act which made murder by witchcraft a crime punishable by death. Agnes was also accused of owning a familiar in the form of a cat named Satan, and, along with her daughter or stepdaughter, Joan, sending a demonic dog to torment 12-year-old Agnes Browne.
2. Rosen, Barbara, *Witchcraft in England 1558–1618,* University of Massachusetts Press, 1991.
3. This turn of events suggests that either Grace had not learned previously from Ursula how to un-witch herself, or that her attempts had been unsuccessful; she may also very likely have been careful to avoid revealing anything to Darcy – who was also her employer – that might incriminate herself in anything that might be construed as witchcraft. Increasingly, 'un-witching' was seen as being as bad as the witchcraft that it presumed to cure, with those in authority growing increasingly suspicious of both. It has also been suggested that Grace had been schooled not to implicate herself by suggesting she had likewise sought the help of a witch to cure her condition.
4. Scouring sand was an abrasive cleaner, used to clean pots and other utensils. Rosen, Barbara, *Witchcraft in England, 1558–1618*, University of Massachusetts Press, Amhurst, 1991, p.109.
5. Gibson, Marion, *Early Modern Witches: Witchcraft Cases in Contemporary Writing*, Routledge, 2005, p.79.
6. *Ibid.* p.79.
7. The identification of a witch by an outside party, in this case a cunning man or woman, was not uncommon, and in many cases played on existing suspicions held by the person who sought out help in the first place. The person consulted often had a working knowledge of local tensions or extracted such information from his or her client, and it is fair to say that in some cases, 'There can be little doubt that such persons encouraged accusations of witchcraft which

121

might otherwise never have been made.' Thomas, *Religion and the Decline of Magic*, p.654.

8. Rosen, p.116.

9. Although the exact age of the child is unknown, the account makes clear that it was less than a year old. Although this may seem fantastical to a modern reader, it clearly did not prevent the 'evidence' of their accusation being taken as proof of Ursula's guilt by Agnes and those who heard her account.

10. As is so often the case, the wife of Cock was conveniently dead by this time and unable to be called in for questioning on the matter. According to Ursula she consulted Cock's wife around the year 1572; the burial registers for Weeley are unfortunately missing due to damage for the period 1568–1576, and as a burial under the name of Cock does not appear after those dates, it can be assumed that the woman died between Ursula consulting her in 1572 and 1576. Intriguingly there appear to be no other entries for the surname for either baptisms, marriages or burials in the years that are available, and it could be speculated that Ursula fabricated the woman and her advice, though there is no firm evidence one way or the other.

11. This word has been variously transcribed as 'charnell', implying the use of corpses and body parts in such magic, or, as pointed out by Barbara Rosen, the more likely given the time and less gruesome option of 'chervil', a herb. Today chervil still has uses and associations with modern witchcraft, in which it is considered to have links to funerals, immortality and contacting spirits.

12. This was most likely St John's Wort, another herb that has been applied over the centuries in such varied uses as curing insanity, treating wounds in battle and dispelling evil spirits. It is still used today as a natural remedy for depression.

13. Rosen, p.113.

14. Whilst the implication of this account was that Alice's spirit or spirits were present and seen by her husband – a more mundane but less incriminating explanation would be that the Newman household suffered from a common problem of the period: rats or mice that were emerging at meal times in the hope of spoils.

15. These matched marks Ursula had on her own body and were taken to be the places where the spirits had sucked at both women, further incriminating them.

16. Rosen, p.127 'Scratching' a witch to draw blood served a two-fold purpose: not only was it thought to identify a witch due to the witch's blood being watery or non-existent, it was also believed that doing so would break the hold of a witch over his or her victim.

17. This is an interesting twist, as witches were often reputed to not be able to cry themselves, a sign of guilt, rather than inflicting this punishment on their

victims. This accusation by Agnes therefore might have done her more harm than it did Ursula.

18. Elizabeth Bennett was also questioned on the matter and seems to have taken Alice Newman's part, refusing to incriminate her other than to say that she had seen Alice be angry with the man when he could not give her the 12 pence she asked for. Not everyone within St Osyth, it seemed, was as willing to throw around accusations of witchcraft and blame as others.

19. It is not clear exactly who else of the accused were transferred with her at this point, or when, but a later visitor to the prison mentioned 'the witches' and it is likely that Alice Hunt and the rest of those to face trial were also taken there around the same time as Ursula or shortly afterwards.

20. Durrant was not the only person to visit Ursula looking for answers; Edward Upcher from Walton visited the prison on 25 March, asking Ursula if his wife was bewitched, and, if so, by whom. Ursula again obliged in providing answers, telling Upcher that it was a woman from their town, with the rather specific description of one of her ears being less than the other, a mole under one of her arms and a large wood-stack in her yard.

21. Rosen, p.137.

22. *Ibid*. p.144.

23. Cockburn, J. S. (ed.) *Calendar of Assize Records: Essex Indictments Elizabeth I*, Her Majesty's Stationary Office, pp.223-4.

24. Although his 'success' in the St Osyth case may have been instrumental in his rise to Sheriff of Essex three years later, Darcy's reputation has not stood the test of time, and it is hard not to agree with with Notestein's remark that 'Justice Darcy was very liberal with his promises of mercy and absolutely unscrupulous about breaking them.' Notestein, *A History of Witchcraft in England from 1558–1718*, p.44.

Although not listed in the official indictments against her, the pamphlet account of the case names Alice Newman as being accused of killing Johnson and his wife and also her own husband. William Newman was still alive around the 10 February 1582, but it is possible that he died between that date and the string of accusations made before Darcy, adding further fuel to the fire.

25. Gibson, *Early Modern Witches*, p.72.

26. Brown, Peter, *Essex Witches*, The History Press, 2014, p.53.

27. As with so many of Murray's examples however, the actual facts of the case do more to refute her argument than support it: in the St Osyth trial there were in fact fourteen or fifteen rather than thirteen women accused in total. Ewen, *Witchcraft and Demonism*, p.59. St Osyth was to feature in witch trials again in the 1640s, when accused from that area were tried under the witch hunts of Matthew Hopkins.

28. Unfortunately the parish registers for St Osyth are not available until 1666, and Bishop's Transcripts go back only as far as 1639, so there is no help to be

gained there regarding the families of the key players in this case or evidence for the origin of Ursula's reputed alias.

29. One later commentator for instance remarks of Ursula that 'Like other women of the sort, she was looked upon with suspicion.' Nottetstein, p.59. There is, however, no evidence to support either the assertion that midwives were persecuted more than any other group of women, or that Ursula was one and was therefore targeted.

30. Harley, David, 'Historians as Demonologists: The Myth of the Midwife-Witch' Social History of Medicine Volume 3, Issue 1 p.1. Like the persistent myth that all English witches were burned, the figure of the persecuted midwife taken to trial as a witch for daring to usurp male authority has been particularly tenacious and damaging to a measured examination of women and the witch trials in general. The book, *Witches, Midwives, and Nurses: A History of Women Healers,* by Barbara Ehrenreich and Deirdre English is a case in point. Although to be applauded for its attempts to redress the balance that is a constant fight for historians of women's and social history, the factual inaccuracies unfortunately do more to cloud the issue than they do to clarify it. The midwife/witch conflation is not solely a modern invention, the seeds of the myth were sown as far back as the fifteenth century in writings of the demonologists, despite the supposed legion of accused midwives being woefully absent from the trial records of the period and beyond.

31. *Ibid.* p.12, and Andrews, Francis, (ed.) *Depositions from the castle of York, relating to offenses committed in the northern counties in the seventeenth century,* Blackwood and Sons, Edinburgh, 1861, p.127. General anxiety regarding midwives *was* in existence and on the increase during the sixteenth century and beyond, and moves to make it a requirement for all midwives to take an oath dates from 1567. The oath in question contained a promise not to use sorcery or enchantment during a woman's labour, a clause that was still present in the second half of the eighteenth century.

32. Barbara Rosen paints a picture of Brian Darcy seizing the opportunity to have his moment in the limelight, an 'ambitious, well-intentioned meddler – one man who finds public duty an excuse for self-dramatisation'. Whether this was a fair assessment or not, Darcy would not have been alone in fitting that description; other Justices of the Peace in the county had already been taken to task by the Privy Council for being overzealous in their attempts to root out witches and witchcraft in their areas. Rosen, pp. 103-4 Darcy's desire to shine and his zeal for persecuting the witches has also been remarked upon. Gibson, p.72.

33. Communities were increasingly coming under pressure from rising poverty and straitened resources; coupled with moves being made to try to put the responsibility for providing relief back on to family and neighbours, economic tensions within many villages were on the rise.

34. Johnson aside, one thing that is strikingly clear from the pamphlet account are the tensions and disagreements that existed within a sixteenth-century community on a day-to-day level. Privacy as we know it today was virtually non-existent, and from the gossip and hearsay contained in the St Osyth account it is all too clear that whether for better or worse, and often thanks to the thinness of the walls, everyone knew what everyone else was doing. The ability to overhear virtually everything that went on in a neighbouring house if you but chose to listen was also instrumental in the spread of accusation and counter-accusation within St Osyth. Alice Newman is referred to as the godmother to Ursula's son, and Elizabeth Bennett's adult son is living with her, both further indications of the close-knit nature of the community in which they lived.

35. It is interesting to note that Richard Ross himself in his examination with Darcy said that he couldn't actually link the Sellis couple to what happened to his barn, other than their son pointing out that it was a 'goodly store of corn'. Either he was led by questions, or he was perhaps covering his own back and letting Darcy make his own connections.

36. Rosen p.115.

37. *Ibid.* p.115.

38. *Ibid.* p.112.

39. With events taking place prior to the 1604 Witchcraft Act, being in possession of or consorting with familiar spirits was not enough in itself to warrant the death sentence on a first offence. Causing death by witchcraft *was* a felony punishable by death under the 1563 Act, and it was for this crime that Ursula Kempe and Elizabeth Bennett went to the noose.

40. Although it is tempting to look for a cause such as poisoned rye and the old favourite ergotism as a cause for the inhabitants of St Osyth hallucinating spirits running around doing harm to each other, there is little evidence to support such a theory and we must therefore stick with equally intriguing but more mundane ideas as to what caused the large number of references to familiar spirits in the accusations and confessions given.

41. Shocking to modern eyes, it was, unfortunately, a not uncommon occurrence, with child testimony being accepted in cases of suspected witchcraft into the seventeenth century. Wallace Notestein holds no punches when he sums up the situation thus: 'The use of evidence in this trial would lead one to suppose that in England no rules of evidence were yet in existence.' Notestein, *A History of Witchcraft in England*, p.44.

42. There is no indication other than the intriguing alias of Grey attributed to Ursula and the child's surname that might give some indication of the identity of the father, an at least one time lover of Ursula, but it is likely that having an illegitimate child went at least some way towards earning her the name of 'naughty'. Although not in itself a guarantee that one would be accused

of witchcraft, when coupled with other factors such as a quarrelsome or outspoken nature and local unrest, it could be and often was something that stood against a woman and was often present in accusations against the accused.

43. The girl's fear of the constables or dislike for her stepmother must have been sufficient enough to override her fear of retribution from Alice, for she told the constables all of this despite the fact Alice had supposedly warned her that if she spoke about them the things themselves would take her away.

44. The revelation of a child saying they had been bidden not to speak of the matter by their parent occurs several times in the St Osyth case, seeming to add further credence to the events being related. The conditions the children were questioned in are unknown and again suspicions of them being led by Darcy and others must be considered. Rather than the children being apparently perfectly happy to incriminate their parents out of vindictiveness, it is entirely and tragically possible that they were told that by corroborating the 'evidence' against them they would actually be helping, and spoke out in full confidence that they would be securing their freedom.

45. Young Agnes gave considerable detail in response to the questions put to her; the cow-shaped familiars had 'little short horns' and they lay on black and white wool in the box in which they were kept. Agnes herself had been given one of these creatures by her mother, a black and white one that she named Crow, and her brother had been given a red and white one named Donne. The cows ate straw and hay, whilst the birds ate wheat, barley, oats, bread and cheese. When asked if the spirits sucked at her mother, Agnes said that they did, and that her brother had likewise seen the blackbird spirits which had sucked his legs. Rosen, p.152.

46. Rosen, p.116.

47. Rosen, p.129 There is no recorded examination for Philip Barrenger other than this brief revelation inserted into the examination of his mother. It is possible that this was a rumour that had circulated in the village and came to Darcy's attention, otherwise it does seem somewhat out of the blue and out of keeping with the other questions being answered. If, as Joan insisted, the matter was entirely innocent, poverty and cold may well have been behind such arrangements.

48. Gordon, Dee, *Infamous Essex Women,* The History Press, 2009, p.??

49. Rosen, p. 120.

50. *Ibid*. p.121.

51. More information on the supernatural elements of the story can be found through the Facebook page for The Cage, St Osyth. Haunted Witch Prison.

52. In actual fact, the nails were a later addition to the scene when the skeletons were exhumed for a second time, and the original bodies were not therefore dealt with in such a fashion.

53. Visitors were charged 6 pence a visit to see the bones that were said to be Ursula's, with the attraction bringing in a not inconsiderable sum over the decade that followed.

54. Details on Ursula and the quest to discover the truth about the origin of the St Osyth skeleton can be found on John Worland's website, and the superb documentary can also be purchased. http://www.ursulakemp.co.uk/history.htm

55. Despite the fact that it is also said that the curving of the spine of one of the skeletons aided in the identification of Ursula, (based upon the trial evidence that she had suffered from 'lameness' which can be interpreted as a form of arthritis) this is not supported by Worland's investigation. The extensive tests prove that the skeleton belonged to an individual in their early twenties, of around 5ft 8in height and was actually a man!

56. The moving ceremony was multi-denominational and included attendance by representatives from the pagan community who, during the journey of 'Ursula' became very interested in the cause and in the woman who met her fate so unjustly.

Chapter 2

1. The Throckmorton children were Jane, Elizabeth, Mary, Grace, Joan and Robert. Intriguingly, another son, Gabriel Throckmorton, is not mentioned in the pamphlet account of the case despite being alive at the time.

2. Despite the pamphlet account asserting that the Throckmortons had not long been in Warboys, the family had in fact been connected to the village for several decades. Robert and Elizabeth Throckmorton had seven of the eight children born to them baptised in the church of St Mary Magdelene, and Robert Throckmorton's father had taken over the lease of the manor house as early as 1540.

3. Rosen, Barbara, (ed.) *Witchcraft in England: 1558–1618*, University of Massachusetts Press, 1991, p.241.

4. *Ibid*. p.243.

5. Gilbert Pickering, the brother of Elizabeth Throckmorton, was a man with a keen interest in witch hunting that may well have added to his desire to visit his nieces to see their condition for himself first-hand.

6. There is no sign of Cicely Burder or anyone else of that surname in the Warboys parish registers, and it is therefore unclear who she was or what role she played in the village. Her fate also remains unknown, though it is hoped that, unlike the Samuels, Cicely might have at least been left in peace once the sorry affair was over. (There is however a Bulmer family in residence in Warboys during the same period, with Agnes and Robert Bulmer baptised to John Bulmer in 1569 and 1574 respectively, along with

a further two Bulmer children in 1578 and 1580 with no father named. It is possible that Burder was a mis-transcription of Bulmer, and that Cicely might have been the wife of John. John Bulmer was also recorded as having drawn blood from John Samuel in the Warboys Court Rolls for 1579.)

7. Rosen, *Witchcraft in England,* p.246.
8. *Ibid.* 247.
9. A fact that was said to be all the more remarkable as Jane had her face turned away from Pickering and therefore could not see that his was not the hand she sought.
10. Matters did not stop there; another of the Throckmorton girls, still in the hallway, had started to echo their sister's ominous words: Cicely Burder was duly presented to the child, who scratched the woman in the same way that Jane had done to Alice.
11. Pickering's home, Titchmarsh Grove, was twenty miles away from Warboys. Almond, Philip, C., *The Witches of Warboys*, I. B Tauris, 2008 p.48.
12. Rosen, p.251.
13. Many more experiments and tests were carried out during Elizabeth's stay in her uncle's household, each one further confirming the belief that she was bewitched and being tormented by both Alice Samuel and the spirits the old woman sent to her. Elizabeth finally returned home 8 September 1590, nearly seven months after she had left, and, despite the wealth of first-hand evidence he had collected of the existence of witchcraft in his diary, one cannot help wondering whether Gilbert Pickering might not have breathed a sigh of relief to be returning his troubled niece to her own home.
14. Unlike on previous occasions, Alice did as she was bidden, unable to refuse due to the fact that she and her husband were tenants of Sir Henry Cromwell himself, making Lady Cromwell the wife of their landlord.
15. Rosen, p.253.
16. *Ibid.* p.253.
17. *Ibid.* p.254.
18. *Ibid.* p.254.
19. *Ibid.* p.256.
20. These things were all apparently proven true whenever someone went to check on Alice, further 'confirming' her guilt and that the spirits spoke the truth.
21. Rosen, p.273.
22. Alice's physical discomfort did not go away, and she complained of pain constantly from that day on for the remainder of her stay in the Throckmorton household.
23. Rosen, p.274.
24. A sceptical reader might find this a convenient turn of events for the Throckmortons if they were determined all along to bring Alice to 'justice' – the Samuel family had, in that case, played right into their hands.

NOTES

25. As an interesting aside, readers are told that, 'One of her neighbours standing by, peradventure better acquainted with her fashions than the rest, said, if they would let her alone, he would be their warrant that she would do well enough.' His prediction was correct, Alice soon again on her feet. Rosen, p. 279.
26. Francis Cromwell and Richard Tryce were also in attendance to hear Alice's words first-hand.
27. Rosen, p.280 This corresponds intriguingly with Alice's previous claim that there was something inside of her and the swelling that was reported one night by Mistress Throckmorton who examined her.
28. *Ibid*. p.281.
29. Although conditions would have been much improved upon from her position in the gaol, the reason for her removal cannot have escaped Agnes, and it is unlikely that she felt more than a momentary relief at her change in circumstances.
30. Rosen, p. 284.
31. Rosen, p.285.
32. *Ibid*. p.286.
33. *Ibid*. p.286.
34. This attack was again far from just a token scratch, but this time 'blood came forth of both sides very abundantly'. Rosen, p.289.
35. That he thought her a fraud was clear, referring to how she had been 'taught her lessons well enough' and making reference to the fact that she was older than 7 and therefore capable of reason – and thus responsible for her own actions and words – though not old enough to legally give evidence in court or be charged as a criminal. Rosen, p.287.
36. Rosen, p.291.
37. Alice told the court that her husband was a witch, but did not likewise incriminate their daughter, maintaining the younger woman's innocence. John Samuel blamed his wife in turn for what had befallen them, saying that it was Alice's fault that they were to go to the gallows.
38. If a woman was proved to be with child the death penalty would be stayed until the time that she gave birth. In theory the sentence was then to be carried out, but, in practice, the condemned could hope to find herself with a commuted sentence or reprieved all together. Benefit of Clergy – being able to recite a verse from the Bible – or sanctuary were specifically removed from those found guilty of witchcraft under the 1563 Act.
39. Almond, p.192.
40. It was reported that Alice made mistakes in both, a fact that is hardly surprising given her situation – indeed it is remarkable in the circumstances that the poor woman managed to recall anything at all.
41. Although Alice was well past caring, it is further to be noted that the indignity was not just witnessed by the gaoler and his wife, but also about forty other people in total.

42. It has been estimated that Alice was between 70 and 80 years of age at the time of her execution, and it has been suggested that Alice might have been a widow when she married John Samuel. The only potential trace of Alice and John Samuel is a marriage record for nearby Upwood in 1561 when an Alice Ibbott married a John Samuel in that year, putting Alice at over 40 at the time of this potentially second marriage.

Intriguingly also there is another Samuel family recorded in the Warboys registers; Robert Samuel and his wife had four children baptised in the church at Warboys: Francis in 1570, Mary in 1575, Elizabeth in 1577, and Joanna in 1580. Although Elizabeth died in early infancy, Francis lived until 1592, dying a few months before the execution of ill-fated Alice and her family, whilst Mary and Joanna were still living at the time Alice Samuel met her end on the gallows. It is possible that Robert Samuel was a brother of John, but without further information to link the two families – and there is no mention of other family members in the pamphlet account – this cannot be verified.

43. The Warboys Court Rolls support this assertion, as at various points throughout the 1570s and 80s, John Samuel was fined for having his cattle stray from his property, for not keeping hedges and ditches in good repair, littering, and the more serious offence of revealing the business of the jury when he was himself serving as a juror.

44. A harsh, abrasive personality and a woman prone to quarrelling is a common occurrence in tales of witchcraft accusations, and it is clear that these undesirable qualities, over time, became part of the stock characteristics of the witch figure. When Henry Pickering and his companions questioned Alice it was said that 'she was very loud in her answers and impatient, not suffering any to speak but herself'. When pressed to practice the womanly virtue of silence, Alice's response was apparently the intriguing, 'born in a mill, begot in a kill, she must have her will'. At their parting, when Pickering lost his temper with her and hoped to see her burned, Alice was equally vociferous in her response, declaring that she would rather see him thrown in the nearby pond, before storming off.

45. Without the means to support herself or to obtain a pricey divorce, Alice would have been left with the stark choices of either killing herself or her husband in order to escape, the latter crime which would have brought her to the same gallows as her condemnation for witchcraft or worse – the punishment for Petty Treason, which husband murder was – was burning at the stake.

46. It must also be remembered that the primary players in bringing Alice to 'justice' were all related to each other; Francis Dorington, the Pickering brothers and the Throckmortons themselves, providing a web of protection and indeed validation around proceedings that the Samuels were powerless to penetrate. Interestingly, it seems that the Samuels may not have been

from the very lowest echelons of society; Anne DeWindt has suggested that John Samuel was of the yeoman class, citing as evidence that he was asked to sit as a juror on several occasions in Warboys and also was one of only seven families in Upwood to be wealthy enough to pay tax in the year 1568 if the Upwood and Warboys couples were indeed one and the same.

47. It must also be remembered that obtaining the execution of a witch was the ultimate way to break the hold over a victim. It was also one of the only theologically sound (albeit extreme) methods of counter magic available to the post-reformation witchcraft victim or relation thereof – scratching, the use of witch bottles and the burning of a witch's hair or nails being considered as bad as the witchcraft originally carried out, even if done in protection. It is at least plausible therefore that, if Robert Throckmorton was intent upon the destruction of the Samuels, it was because he genuinely believed it was the only way to guarantee the relief of his daughters.

48. There is nothing said about those who may have doubted the veracity of the Throckmortons' claims, apart from those doubts voiced by the Samuels themselves, but that is hardly surprising given the biased nature of the account in the Throckmortons' favour.

49. Rosen p.230 Rosen also points out that this explanation is problematic as the servants who shared the symptoms with the Throckmorton girls were 'cured' upon leaving the house, and the girls themselves ceased to suffer immediately after the Samuels were executed. There is also the fact that neither Master or Mistress Throckmorton nor their sons experienced any of the symptoms suffered by the rest of the household.

50. Not to be confused with 'obsession' where the spirit exerted influence externally rather than residing within the afflicted person. As the story progressed there were several spirits who entered proceedings – Pluck, Catch, White, Blue, Smack, Hardname, Smack, (Smack's cousin), Smack (another cousin of the first Smack) and Callico.

51. Bernard, Richard, *A Guide to Grand-jury Men*, London, 1627 pp 49-51. Bernard also, importantly, listed ways in which to tell if the seemingly possessed was faking their symptoms or not.

52. Well established by the seventeenth century, in part due to the influence of the Warboys case, in the high-profile case of the Belvoir witches, Joan Flower and her daughters were said to have bewitched the sons of Earl and Lady Rutland after being unable to harm the couple directly.

53. It must be remembered that belief in the existence of the Devil was very real to all in the sixteenth century, and therefore the idea that Satan or his minions could afflict a person was wide-spread.
    As a result of such beliefs, it was therefore necessary for there to be a cure for those who found themselves possessed, and such was provided by the medieval church in the form of exorcisms, when the spirit was commanded to

leave the victim by a priest as part of a complex ritual. For later advocates of reform, this was all superstitious nonsense, and under the reformed church it was declared that the possessed now needed to put their faith in God, seeking recourse in prayer and fasting and to hope for the best. This was far from reassuring to those who had previously relied on the power of the priesthood to drive away the demons that threatened to torment their souls and bodies, and indeed there had been a steady increase in the number of recorded cases of possession in England since the reformation of the mid-sixteenth century, a direct reflection of increased anxiety over the matter.

54. This is also reflected in the incident that occurred after Alice returned to the manor house after collecting something from home – the condition of the girls might not have improved as it had previously in Alice's presence, but this was made up for by the fact that the girls could now only communicate through Alice and no other, thus maintaining and tightening their control over the old woman.

55. Also, it must be remembered that, conveniently, the girls were said to be deprived of their senses during a fit, and it is likely that the adults around them grew used to speaking more plainly in their presence, thinking them unable to understand or hear them, than they would have done in normal circumstances, allowing not only for further ammunition to be gained against Alice, but also to help them keep their stories straight.

56. Almond, pp 88-9.

57. Rosen p.251, Almond, p.81.

58. This theory is supported somewhat by the fact that the servants who left the house immediately recovered, as if their minds had cleared, and has also been used as an explanation for several other cases of mass possession, including the later Salem Witch Trials.

59. Almond, p.73.

60. It was not only theologically unsound, Richard Bernard in his advice to jury men spoke against it, as did several other commentators of the time, declaring it to be both illegal and serving no valid purpose.

61. Almond, p.40.

62. This motif continued into the eighteenth century, and beyond, and was again used as proof of witchcraft in the case of Jane Wenham against the young Anne Thorn, who, interestingly, behaved in much the same fashion as the Throckmorton daughters. There are also many instances of it in nineteenth century newspaper accounts, and scratching seems to have been one of the most enduring pieces of witch-lore.

63. Under the Act causing death by bewitchment was punishable by death, tormenting or causing illness through witchcraft brought a term of imprisonment if for a first offence.

64. Unlike the apparently motiveless attack against the Throckmorton girls, Alice was seen to have clear cause for taking her revenge on Lady Cromwell after

the woman accused her of bewitching Jane and her sisters and also cut her hair and took her hairnet into the bargain. This unfortunately made the indictment all the more believable to those present in the courtroom and reading the Throckmorton-biased pamphlet account after Alice's death.

65. Robert Throckmorton took his family to Ellington, Huntingdonshire, though he himself returned to Warboys eventually as he was buried there at his death.

66. It has been suggested that Elizabeth Throckmorton, Robert Throckmorton's wife, was dead before the family left Warboys, but there is nothing to substantiate this within the Warboys burial registers for the period.

67. Ellis, Sir Henry, *The Visitation of the County of Huntingdon*, 1849, Camden Society, London, p.124.

68. Almond, p.36.

Chapter 3

1. Gibson, p.182.
2. There has been speculation over the years regarding the origin of this nickname for the matriarch of the Whittle family. One explanation is that it stemmed from 'Chatterbox', due to the woman's habit of muttering to herself. As satisfying a theory as this may be, unfortunately the term chatterbox was only in use from the last quarter of the eighteenth century and therefore cannot have been the origin of the name. William Bennett also speculates that it comes from a corruption or variation of the surname Chadwick which might hold up better under scrutiny.
3. A rood is a now unused measurement that equates to between 5 and 7.3 metres, putting the distance James refers to at between 50 and 73 metres away.
4. In the account, the charming and evocative term 'day gate' is used to refer to this time of day.
5. Gibson, p.187.
6. *Ibid.* p.187.
7. *Ibid.* p.188.
8. Gibson, p.285 Elsons refers to awls. A later description of what ailed John Law is instructive in suggesting what might have actually happened; it sounds like a stroke.

'John Law the Pedler, before his unfortunate meeting with this witch, was a very able sufficient stout man of body, and a goodly man of stature. But by this devilish art of witchcraft his head is drawn awry, his eyes and face deformed, his speech not well to be understood; his thighs and legs stark/struck lame: his arms lame especially the left side, his hands lame and turned out of their course, his body able to endure no travel.' Gibson, p. 246.

9. As highlighted by several commentators, it is interesting how the details of the story subtly change from retelling to retelling; Abraham Law's version is the only one that involves his father giving the pins despite Alizon's inability to pay for the pins requested.

10. It is highly probable that this other, older, woman was meant to be Old Demdike, yet more evidence against her.

11. One cannot help but wonder whether this account had at least some basis in fact; it is possible that Old Demdike experienced an illness during this time or was otherwise unwell, and this was now being reinterpreted either to make sense of it herself or in order to fit the questioning she was faced with. It is also possible that these events occurred in the half world between wakefulness and sleep, the encounter with the dog spirit being a particularly vivid and frightening dream.

12. Gibson, p.183 These words, if reported accurately, are of great interest, as they reflect both popular belief (i.e. the conflation of memories of the burning of heretics with current executions of witches) and actual fact – witches in England were hanged not burned.

13. *Ibid.* p.183.

14. The charm is recounted in full in the text, as follows:
Three biters hast thou bitten,
the heart, ill eye, ill tongue:
three bitter shall be thy boot,
Father, Son, and Holy Ghost
a Gods name
Five Pater-nosters, five Avies,
and a Creed,
In worship of the five wounds of our Lord.
Gibson, p.196.

15. *Ibid.* p.188.

16. Thomas Covell was a well known figure in Lancaster, serving not only as Keeper of the Castle for a period of forty-eight years from 1591 until his death in 1639, but also as Mayor on six occasions and in the role of coroner. There are conflicting reports on his personality, with the Rev. Henry Burton referring to him as a 'beastly man' after his imprisonment under him in 1637, whilst others provide a more positive picture. Covell had rooms in the castle, and, if the 'plot' were indeed fact rather than fiction, it is likely that he was intended to meet his death in the planned explosion. Today, Covell is remembered by the Covell Cross, a monument that stands outside his former rooms at the Judges' Lodgings in Lancaster where he lived and died.

17. Jennet Preston was also apprehended, and taken to York Castle where she was held and questioned before going to trial.

18. Chattox was indicted for killing Richard Nutter by witchcraft. Her daughter, Anne Redferne, for the same against Christopher Nutter. Elizabeth Device was indicted for the murder of John and James Robinson, and in helping her mother and Alice Nutter to kill Henry Mitton. James had bewitched Anne Townley to death, along with John Duckworth, and John and Blaze Hargrieves. Alison Device had lamed and consumed the body of John Law, the pedlar already mentioned. Alice Nutter and Katherine Hewit were also indicted for murder by witchcraft, whilst John and Jane Bulcock were accused of the only slightly lesser crime of using their witchcraft to drive Jennet Deane to madness and waste her body.

    There was also a further group of suspected witches tried at the same assizes, known as the Salmesbury Witches; they had been accused by a 14-year-old girl named Grace Sowerbutts of child murder, attending sabbats and various acts of maleficium, but Grace eventually confessed that she had fabricated her story at the behest of a Catholic priest.

19. Gibson, p.199. This harangue against Elizabeth Device is interesting as before this point it has been Demdike herself rather than her daughter who had been painted as the worst witch of them all. It is very likely that, with Demdike being dead and the courts cheated of their victim, Elizabeth became the most obvious and natural candidate for a replacement figure of evil.

20. There is some debate regarding Jennet's actual age at the time of the trial; although the pamphlet states that she was 9 years old, argument has been made for her being somewhat older and around 11 or 12 when she gave evidence against her family.

21. There is again further evidence of Elizabeth Device being placed in the starring role in the absence of her mother; the account states that 'because I have charged her to be the principle agent, to procure a solemn meeting at Malkin Tower of the Grand Witches, to consult of some speedy course for the deliverance of her mother, Old Demdike, her daughter, and other witches at Lancaster: the speedy execution of Master Covell, little suspected or deserved any such practice or villany against him: the blowing up of the castle, with divers other wicked and devilish practices and murders.' before going to on relate almost gleefully the 'evidence' given against her. Gibson p.203-4.

22. Gibson, p.206.

23. The full list of indictments is as follows: Chattox, bewitching Robert Nutter to death. Elizabeth Device three counts of murder by witchcraft, John and James Robinson and Henry Mytton. James Device, bewitching Anne Townely, John Duckworth and John and Blaze Hargrieves to death. Anne Redferne for bewitching Robert Nutter to death along with her mother. She was not found guilty of this, but her second trial for bewitching Christopher Nutter to death she was found guilty and condemned. Alice Nutter bewitching Henry

Mytton to death. John and Jane Bulcock, bewitching Jennett Deane until she went mad. Katherine Hewit bewitching Anne Foulds to death. Alizon Device, bewitching John Law, Margaret Pearson bewitched Dodgesons mare, Isobel Robey, unspecified witchcraft.

24. Despite being recorded by Potts in the pamphlet account as having been acquitted, John and Jane Bulcock met the same fate as Alizon Device and the others and were hanged.

25. The Salmsebury witches, tried at the same time, were acquitted.

26. Gibson, p.191.

27. Gibson, p.199.

28. Gibson, p.202.

29. Ewen, Witchcraft and Demonism, p.213.

30. As it transpired, Robert Nutter was not able to carry out his threat as he died on his way home from Wales; yet further evidence some would say of the witchcraft performed against him by Anne Redferne and her mother.

31. The way in which Chattox especially, and also Demdike, were said to terrorise their locality is striking. There is a theory that this was the only way they could – being poor, economically and socially low – actually get anything close to what they felt was what they deserved and needed. Thomas p.674-5.

32. Thomas, p.612. The lives of the queen and her counsellors were believed to have been in danger from enemies using such magic; rather than being considered out-dated superstition, the threat was investigated and taken very seriously indeed.

33. Gibson, p.232.

34. Gibson, p.182.

35. Gibson, p.199.

36. In both the Lancaster case and that of Jennet Preston in York, the moment the cases turned fully against the accused came when James and Jennet gave their damning evidence to Nowell regarding the meeting at Malkin Tower, and thus they led to the execution of those found guilty in both instances. Indeed, Jennet was actually instrumental in the condemnation of Jennet Preston, as it was due to the evidence collected from herself and her brother James regarding her attendance at the meeting at Malkin Tower that was then related to the jury at York who tried Jennet Preston, and subsequently condemned her to death. James Device also played his part, and was taken by yeoman Henry Hargrieves to Gisburn to identify Jennet Preston as one of the women who had been present at the fateful meeting of the witches. Pumfrey, Stephen, Potts, plots and politics: 'James I's Daemonologie and The Wonderful Discoverie of Witches', pp.20-25, Lumby, Jonathan, 'Those to whom evil is done': family dynamics in the Pendle witch trials', p.60 in Poole, Robert, (ed.) *The Lancashire Witches, Histories and Stories*, Manchester University Press, Manchester, 2002, p.20

NOTES

37. Bennett, Walter, *The Pendle Witches*, Lancashire County Council, Lancashire, 1985, p.6, and Lumby, Jonathan, 'Those to whom evil is done' in (ed.) Poole, Robert, *The Lancashire Witches*, Manchester University Press, 2002, p.64.

38. Cobban believes that his condition might have been due to torture by the gaoler rather than a pre-existing condition, taking as evidence the fact that Covell was noted to have taken 'very great pains' to discover what James knew. Cobban, Jennie Lee, *The Lure of the Lancashire Witches*, p.12. Although torture in the formal sense was, unlike on the Continent, illegal under the English legal system of the time, mistreatment could and did occur in prisons to varying degrees.

39. Bennett, *The Pendle Witches*, p.6. Ewen agrees with this assessment, likewise referring to Jennet as precocious, and numerous sources repeat such judgements of the girl. Ewen, Witchcraft and Demonism, p.214.

40. Gibson, p.264.

41. This 'proof' of Jennet's honesty has not always been met with approval; William Bennett pointing out that it was 'an artifice that any child of normal intelligence would have immediately have recognised as a trap'. Bennett p.5.

42. Gibson, p.210.

43. Gibson, pp.101-2.

44. Lumby, p.89.

45. Cobban, p.151 If true, this puts a rather chilling spin on the events that followed.

46. Gibson, p.264.

47. Cobban, Jennie Lee, *The Lure of the Lancashire Witches*, Palatine Books, 2011, p.98 It is interesting to see the same family names involved in both the 1612 and 1634 cases. In another potential twist of fate, it was a man named John Robinson who had made accusations against Elizabeth Device all those years ago; was he a relation of the Edmund Robinson who saw witches two decades later? Also, the whether stolen and killed for the feast at Malkin Tower had belonged to another Robinson, this one from Barley.

48. If this woman was indeed the Jennet who condemned her family, it would be interesting to know how she had spent the years that followed the execution of her family. If one and the same, she had clearly remained in the area, although the keeping of her maiden surname suggests she had not married. It would be intriguing to know how she was viewed by the community in which she lived and any remaining peripheral family such as her uncle and aunt. There is further evidence to favour this second Jennet as the one from the 1612 case, as during the first trial, it came to light that one of Elizabeth Device's supposed victims had accused her of having had a bastard child with a man named Sellar. A further argument against the Jennet arrested in 1633 being the same as the Pendle witness is that in one version of the pamphlet detailing the later case, Jennet is

listed as 'Jennett, wife of William Davis', thus making Davis/Device her married and not her maiden name. Gibson p.245.

49. There seems to be some confusion regarding Nowell's age; one source gives his age as 62 in 1612, whilst others put the Justice as being 30 years of age at the time of the trial. Genealogical evidence supports the latter, and Nowell died in 1623 at the age of 41.

50. Ewen, *Witchcraft and Demonism*, p.214. Although both judges are often presented in a negative light, in a twist James Sharpe points out that the St Osyth case could have resulted in as many executions as occurred at Pendle, if not for, rather than despite, Darcy's involvement. Sharpe, James, 'Introduction: the Lancashire witches in historical context,' in (ed.) Poole, Robert, *The Lancashire Witches*, p.8.

51. Rosen, p.357.

52. Bennett, *The Pendle Witches*, p.5.

53. Lumby for one makes the valid point that Nowell's Protestantism did not automatically of itself make him inclined to root out witches. Sharpe, James, Introduction, in Poole, (ed.) *The Lancashire Witches,* p.8. There are also several examples of Justices and magistrates erring on the side of leniency or, increasingly, throwing out a case altogether. Also it has been suggested that 'Whatever the role of judges and inquisitors may have been on the Continent, it cannot be said that in England the judiciary ever took much initiative in the prosecution of witches.' Thomas p.546.

54. Ewen, *Witchcraft and Demonism*, p.213. Sharpe, in Poole, (ed.) *The Lancashire Witches,* p.2.

55. Complaints about Demdike and Chattox had gone back some years, and if Chattox had exhorted tribute from John Device, the husband of a friend, then what further bribes and bargains did she have going on with others, and what power did she hold over these victims?

56. Sharpe, in Poole, (ed.) *The Lancashire Witches,* pp.8-9.

57. Despite his supposed success in the Starkie case, Darrel was later tried and imprisoned on charges of deceit and counterfeiting after his more spectacular and, some might say, unwise, connections with the Boy of Burton and William Somers.

58. Lumby, Jonathan, 'Those to whom evil is done', in (ed.) Poole, Robert, *The Lancashire Witches*, Manchester University Press, 2002, p.66.

59. Jennet's tale is particularly tragic. She had been initially brought to trial at the Lent Assizes at York in 1612 by accusations from Thomas Lister regarding the murder by witchcraft of the child of someone named Dodgson. She was acquitted, only to be found guilty of the murder of Thomas Lister senior – to whom Jonathan Lumby speculates she might have been mistress – and condemned and hanged for it. Even at the time, many people believed the charges against Jennet to have been maliciously motivated and that she was innocent.

NOTES

60. Sir Edward was created a Baron of the Exchequer in 1610 and was a prominent lawyer, judge and landowner.
61. Pumfrey, Stephen, Potts, plots and politics, in (ed.) Poole, Robert, *The Lancashire Witches*, p.31.
62. Ewen, *Witchcraft and Demonism*, p.128.
63. Thomas, *Religion and the Decline of Magic*, p.576.
64. Bennett, *The Pendle Witches*, p.5.
65. Sharpe, in Poole, (ed.) p.9.
66. Gibson, p.255.
67. *Ibid*. p.254.
68. Lumby, Jonathan, *The Lancashire Witch Craze: Jennet Preston and the Lancashire Witches*, 1612, Carnegie, 1995 p.63.
69. *Ibid*. p.63-4. Whatever the cause of his start of witchcraft prosecution, Bromley was still going strong some seven years later when he presided over the trial of the Belvoir Witches, a trial which again resulted in the execution of the accused.
70. Ewen, Witchcraft and Demonism, p.216.
71. Sharpe, in Poole, (ed.) p.13.
72. Interestingly, this does not mean Christopher Nutter did not believe in witchcraft; far from it, merely that he did not think it a viable explanation in the given situation.
73. Lumby, in Poole, (ed.) p.67.
74. Bennett, for instance, states that the young woman believed she had actually caused John Law harm, and that with her background of 'living in wretched poverty with a blind old grandmother, a badly disfigured mother and a subnormal brother' it was only natural that she would come to that conclusion as she didn't know better or otherwise. Bennett, p.10.
75. Gibson, p.3.
76. Rosen, p.357.
77. As the robbery took place before Alizon's meeting with John Law, if true, this series of events would take precedence as a cause over the meeting with the pedlar. Bennett also suggests that the robbery took place not, as is commonly held, in 1601, but in the year of the trial, 1612, using this to give further weight to his theory.
78. There were a variety of beliefs relating to the communion bread; it could be used for anything from charming a garden against caterpillars to curing blindness or a fever. Thomas, p.38.
79. *Ibid*. p.39.
80. The creature, in the shape of a hare, was not best pleased, and 'the said thing threatened to pull this examinate in pieces'. Gibson p.208. On this occasion, James saved himself by marking himself with the sign of the cross – a Catholic sign and in itself counted as much of a superstition such as others were trying to stamp out regarding the communion.

81. Furthermore, Potts paid tribute to Sir Thomas Knyvet, (Baron Escrick, Privy Councillor and favourite of James I) in his account of the case: It was Knyvett who discovered Guy Fawkes in the cellars of parliament in 1604. Pumfrey, in Poole, (ed.) p.36-7.

82. *Ibid.* pp 37-8 Stephen Pumfrey speculates that it is more likely that these particular details were embellished or outright invented by Nowell and his fellow Justice, with the potentially unstable James Device agreeing to what was suggested under questioning. One pertinent question is where would the assembled 'witches' have found gunpowder in the required quantity in the first place?

83. Bennett, p.18.

84. Pumfrey, in Poole, p.32.

85. Gibson, p233.

86. Despite this, Potts makes much of Alice's rich state and good nature, and also that Bromley took pains to make sure that she was tried fairly. 'Great was the care and pains of his Lordship, to make trial of the innocencie of this woman,' before going on to add that 'it is very certain she was of the grand counsel at Malkin Tower upon Good Friday, and was there present, which was a very great argument to condemn her.' *Ibid.* p.233. Rather than being the mistress at Roughlee Hall – a fiction started by James Crossley in his 1845 introduction to Potts's account, and perpetuated by two popular novels on the Pendle case over the following century – Alice was actually the wife of Richard Nutter, a 'moderately wealthy' yeoman, living in a farmhouse at Crowtrees, Roughlee. Ellen Hartley was actually mistress at Roughlee Hall at the time of the Pendle witch trial. Whittaker, Gladys, *Roughlee Hall: Fact and Fiction*, Marsden Antiquarians, 1980, pp 4-5.

87. Bennett, p.28.

88. Cobban, p.147. Although it is highly unlikely to be the actual grave of the executed witch, the tradition is an enduring one, speaking much of the deep-seated desire to have physical and tangible connections with the past..

89. Interestingly, and a testament to the popularity and enduring nature of the subject matter, *The Lancashire Witches* is the only one of Ainsworth's forty published novels to have remained permanently in print since its first edition.

90. One of several great departures from the historical record in Ainsworth's *The Lancashire Witches* is the discovery that Alizon Device is actually the long-lost lovechild of Alice Nutter, adding a whole new twist to an already sensational set of events.

Chapter 4

1. The usual pattern of accusations in English witchcraft cases involved relatively small numbers, compared to areas of Europe where whole towns and villages could be almost wiped out by the end of a period of persecution.

2. Despite the often quoted over-inflated figures, the number of recorded executions for witchcraft in England actually numbered under 300 in total for the entire period 1560–1736. It is unclear exactly how many of those occurred at the instigation of Hopkins and his associates, but what cannot be denied is that a large portion of these were carried out under their influence, and that the terror and persecution that they inspired and fostered amongst the communities they entered is heartbreakingly clear.

3. Geographically the accused at Bury St Edmunds are interesting because the condemned (not to mention those who faced trial but were found not guilty) came from several villages and towns. It therefore reflects a series of smaller, local tensions and situations coming together to form a larger widespread case. Most of the eighteen witches came from Halesworth, Chattisham and Copdock, and there were known social and familial connections between those in the areas, adding to and enlarging a web of fear, suspicion and accusation that allowed the persecution to perpetuate itself.

4. This was most likely Almoner's Barn in Bury St Edmunds, a place that sometimes doubled as a pest house and was owned by the corporation of the town. Gaskill, Malcolm, *Witchfinders: A Seventeenth-Century English Tragedy*, John Murray, 2005, p.156.

5. The prisoners' pact and the rejection of it was referred to by John Stearne in his work a few years later, where he wrote how at Bury St Edmunds

> ... when there were eighteen to be executed; most of them kept in a barn together, they made a covenant amongst themselves, not to confess a word next day at the gallows, when they were to be hanged, notwithstanding they had formerly confessed, and some of them after they came into the gaol, and some before the Bench and Country, but most of them (if not all) before the Justices of the Peace, and so died the next day accordingly very desperately, except one penitent woman which refused their covenant, or agreement: so she made it known, and how they made a singing of a psalm after they had done it.

Stearne, John, *A Confirmation and Discovery of Witchcraft*, London, 1648. It would be intriguing to know the identity of this outspoken woman and what her motives were for objecting so vehemently to the rest of the condemned maintaining their silence and lack of further confession. Perhaps she truly believed she had done as she had confessed – whatever that was – and feared putting her soul in danger by taking back whatever she had uttered. It is also possible that she blamed those around her for her situation, seeing her associates and perhaps neighbours as responsible for her condemnation.

6. Although eighteen people initially went to the gallows, there were in fact reported to be at least 120 further suspected witches in prison at Bury St

Edmunds at the time awaiting trial, and there are various estimates as to how many were finally executed.

7. Given revised estimates in recent decades of the number of executions that took place in England, 200 in one area over the space of a few weeks is unlikely. There is no firm reason to discredit outright Stearne's opinion regarding the sixty-eight, although it is unknown how many of these actually went to the gallows. (A total of 117 condemned is named by Richard Deacon, but, given his known proclivity for exaggeration and outright fabrication, this figure should, as with much of his work, be taken with a pinch of salt. What *is* clear is that events at Bury St Edmunds, as elsewhere, were a terrible tragedy.)

8. Notestein, Wallace, *A History of Witchcraft in England, 1558–1718*, 1911 p.393.

9. Ewen, *Witchcraft and Demonism*, p.188 Handily, Gyles convicted Olive with the assertion that he had served her for twenty years, and that 'Doll' had sent him to kill Joan. Joan likewise named Olive as her tormentor, and the old woman was accordingly found guilty and executed.

10. Gaskill, *Witchfinders*, p.138.

11. *Ibid.* p.139.

12. In fact, what remains remarkable is that this unpopular man managed to remain in his post for half a century when faced with such great opposition and concerted attempts to remove him by those in his flock. By contrast, the vicar of Great Clacton, Joseph Long, used the changing of the times to get himself back into the good books of his parishioners. Much disliked and maligned for his behaviour and opinions, he took advantage of the witch hunting fervour that had gripped the area and launched a campaign against the Cooper family who were suspected and greatly disliked.

13. Anne Ansom or Annsom is often erroneously cited as having been executed in 1645 as part of the main Bury St Edmunds trial, but there is no evidence that she was amongst this number, events involving her having taken place several decades previous.

14. Prior to this, Cooke had made the allegations that when his son was sick Lowes had used a charm in the form of a golden chain to help make him better – when the 'cure' was successful, instead of showing gratitude, Cooke insisted this proved Lowes' witchcraft. Not only that, Lowes has appeared, Cooke insisted, in his room in the night, further tormenting him. Lowes launched a slander suit in response, and Cooke was forced to pay damages and costs to just shy of £30.

15. Anon, *A Magazine of Scandall. Or, A Heap of wickedness of two infamous Ministers*, London, 1642.

16. *Ibid.*

17. *Ibid.* A4.

18. If the account is to be believed, Lowes was also able to play the long game; a local tailor, painted as poor, honest and unassuming, evaded Lowes for the space of two years before the wily minister finally managed to trap him. Having got into the man's good graces by making himself 'familiar and loving to the tailor', Lowes had, with the good relationship established, sent for the tailor one Sunday morning whilst he himself was still in bed. He needed his breeches mended, the vicar said, so that he could wear them that day. The tailor accordingly did as he was asked, only to find himself in court, cited by Lowes for breaking the law – it was unlawful to mend clothes on a Sunday!

19. This was a particularly grievous offence given the uncertainty of the times, it could be a matter of life or death to know which side someone was on during a conflict where even close family members fought on opposite sides.

20. *A Magazine of Scandall*, A5.

21. *Ibid* A5.

22. *Ibid* A6. This might, if believed, go some way to explain why his parishioners had been so far unable to remove Lowes from his post. To further reinforce the image of Lowes as dangerous and unlawful, the author goes on to gleefully relate how he was also guilty of treasure seeking; silver spoons had been lost and in order to attempt to recover them for his own use, Lowes had sent for help from one called Woolward, 'a notorious reputed conjuror'. By the 1604 Witchcraft Act and those that had been passed before it, attempting to recover lost goods through magical means was a criminal offence, in Lowes' day punishable by imprisonment and four turns in the pillory for a first offence, and death for a subsequent conviction.

23. Just in case anyone might have doubts, several volunteers who were known to be innocent threw themselves into the water as proof that the judgement was correct. It didn't go quite as planned, as they too floated rather than sinking as those who were innocent were supposed to do!

24. Ewen, *Witchcraft and Demonism*, p.291, *Notes and Queries*, 21 March 1896, p.233.

25. Nathanial Man testified that after he had got a warrant against Lowes, the minister had given his wife money to be able to feed their child. After this seeming act of kindness, the child had fallen ill, slowly fading away until it died. Daniel Rayner also testified that Lowes had confessed to causing the death of many cattle and using his yellow imp to cause great mischief at sea. Ewen, *Witchcraft and Demonism*, p.291.

26. Stearne, *A Confirmation and Discovery of Witchcraft*, p.24.

27. Hutchinson, Francis, *An Historical Essay Concerning Witchcraft*, London, 1718, pp.66-9.

28. This is one of the reasons for the huge disparity between the conviction and execution rates in England and the rest of Europe; an estimated 60,000 executions compared with England's under 300 for the same period.

29. *A True Relation of the Arraignment of Eighteen Witches*, p.6.
30. Ewen, *Witch Hunting and Witch Trials*, p.308.
31. *Ibid*. p.295. In this case at least reason won out and the crime was not ultimately laid at Anne Marsh's door, the bill against her being declared 'ignoramus' by the jury.
32. It seems that two to three days was the average time suspects were watched for; not out of any humanitarian concerns, but more because this was how long it took for a sleep deprived and exhausted man or woman to break down and confess to the satisfaction of those who watched them. John Stearne put the upper limit at four days in his reference to waking in his pamphlet, though it was recorded that Margaret Powell didn't confess until six days had passed.
33. Hopkins, p.2. Stearne likewise refers to the names Grizzel and Greedigut as two separate familiars belonging to Joan Wallis of Keyston in Huntingdonshire; it is tempting to suggest that these might have been put into her mouth by her questioners rather than being of her own invention. Stearne, p.13.
34. Stearne, p.27.
35. *Ibid*. p.15.
36. *Ibid*. p.16. With this in particular, it would be incredibly interesting to know exactly what, if anything, was actually observed by Hopkins, Stearne and those who watched Elizabeth Clarke with them. Did the animals in question enter the place where she was held and they were taken to be the imps that she said they were? Or was nothing seen at all, the whole being an invention after the fact to justify the means the witch hunters were using to achieve their ends? It is another one of the tantalising questions that will never be satisfactorily answered, but which continues to echo through the centuries as we try our hardest to understand what went on during these confusing, tempestuous and often violent times.
37. *Ibid*. p.45.
38. *Ibid*. p.53.
39. *Ibid*. p50. He had corroboration from a suspected witch herself, as Elizabeth Clarke had apparently told her questioners that everyone who had marks were witches and that most of those also had familiars.
40. Stearne, p.45.
41. *Ibid*. p.45.
42. *Ibid* p.27.
43. *Ibid*. p.27.
44. *Ibid*. p.5.
45. *Ibid*. p.5. 'For Satan appeareth not to them in any shape until he find some perpearedness … So you may find as I said before, extreme poverty, passionate sorrow accompanied with solitariness, too much enraged with anger and desire of revenge…' Stearne, p.33.
46. Ewen, *Witchcraft and Demonism*, p.295.

47. *Ibid.* p.297.

48. *Ibid.* p.298.

49. Ewen, Witchcraft and Demonism, p.285.

50. There was very likely something of a self-fulfilling prophecy taking place; Hopkins and Stearne observed what they saw to be a trend, which was then reproduced and continued, their leading questions in turn producing the results that they expected from their suspects.

51. Elizabeth Clarke, the first witch Hopkins was involved in bringing to justice, related how she had let the Devil know her carnally, and that he was 'a tall, proper, black haired gentleman', adding the snub that he was 'a properer man than yourself'. It may indeed have been Clarke's confession that inspired leading questions against further suspects when Hopkins and Stearne reached Suffolk, and the unusual frequency of sex with the Devil into the Bury St Edmunds narrative.

52. Ewen, Witchcraft and Demonism, p.282. This was a common complaint against the Devil and his love making from confessions of the time; he was often described as cold and the experience of coupling was generally related to have not been a pleasant one. Anne Boreham from Sudbury likewise related how the Devil had been 'heavier and colder than any man' when he came to her in bed. Ewen, p.284.

53. *Ibid.* p.283, p.286.

54. Stearne, p.38. Rebecca West witnessed a meeting of her mother's 'confederates' before she herself was suckled by imps, sealed a covenant with her own blood, and took part in a marriage ceremony with the Devil himself.

55. *Ibid.* p.292.

56. *Ibid.* p.292.

57. *Ibid.* p.298. Sussums was lucky; although he confessed to being sucked by imps, he was discharged and was still living until at least 1648.

58. Anon, *A True Relation of the Arraignment of Eighteen Witches*, London, 1645, p.7.

59. Anne also admitted that she sometimes worked alone. Three years ago she had sent her grey imp to kill Elizabeth, daughter of Robert Kirk of Maningtree; her victim had languished for a year and then died. The reason behind this act of vengeance was that Anne had asked Elizabeth for money but had been refused. Anne had further exacted revenge when, on being evicted from her farm the widow Rawlins was put into it instead in her place. For this slight, Anne had sent her grey imp to kill Rawlins' daughter. She had, Anne insisted, little choice but to send the imps out to do their mischief; if she did not, then she herself suffered, growing greatly ill – on the contrary, she was well and healthy when the imps were out and about causing mayhem at her behest. For sustenance, the creatures sucked from the teats that were concealed in or near her private parts, and in turn they often spoke to her in a hollow voice and told

her that she would never feel the torments of hell. Needless to say, Anne Leech met her end on the gallows.

60. Interestingly the belief that witchcraft ran in families is also prominent in other trials that claimed relatively large number of accusations and executions, noticeably the previously highlighted case of the Pendle Witches.
61. Stearne, p.8.
62. *Ibid.* p.33.
63. Wright, p.32.
64. Henry Carre from Suffolk died in gaol during the three week adjournment, with Stearne recording that 'he died in gaol at that time'. Stearne p.25. Although disease is one explanation for this, it is also possible – especially given the age of some of those being held – that their rough treatment, despite the protests of Hopkins and Stearne to the contrary – was at least in part responsible for their demise.
65. Stearne, p.34.
66. Gaskill, p.123.
67. Stearne, p.14-15.
68. Gaskill, pp. 78-9.
69. *The Moderate Intelligencer*, 4-11 September, 1645 p.1.
70. *Ibid* p.1. Interestingly, this point had been addressed by Richard Bernard in his *A guide to Grand Jurymen* with respect to Witches of 1627. According to Bernard, the Devil recruited women rather than men because, being of a more credulous nature, it was easier to mislead and deceive them. They were also more prone to revenge and malice due to being superstitious and impatient, which again made them more desirable for the Devil's purposes. They were better placed to spread witchcraft and dissent to others, as less likely to be able to guard their tongues. Finally they suffered from the sin of pride, meaning they thought themselves able to command others, and again more pliable to commanding spirits than men.
71. Talking of his gathering of experience and expertise in trying witches, Hopkins asserts that he 'never travelled far for it, but in March 1644 he had some seven or eight of that horrible sect of witches living in the town where he lived, a town in Essex called Manningtree, with diverse other adjacent witches of other towns, who every six weeks in the night (being always on the Friday night) had their meeting close by his house, and had their several solemn sacrifices there offered to the Devil.' One night Hopkins had heard one of the witches speaking with her imps and had himself seen to her apprehension; the woman was searched by women 'who had for many years known the Devil's marks' and discovered to have several teats. Hopkins, Matthew, *A Discovery of Witches*, London, 1647, p.2.
72. Hopkins, *A Discovery*, p.5. Needless to say, this claim is highly suspect and a classic example of the way both Hopkins and Stearne attempted to gloss over

and distance themselves from the excesses of what took place, largely, at their behest.

73. Stearne, *A Confirmation,* p.2.

74. Hopkins took his argument even further with a good dose of victim blaming, pointing out that if there were those who still didn't sleep despite the fact they were offered it, *he* could hardly be blamed for their stubbornness!

75. This somewhat contradicts his own previous assertion that the aim of waking and walking was to encourage the familiars to come to the witch and therefore reveal themselves.

76. The wording is indeed interesting, as he doesn't say he didn't do it, just that no proof could be found, which is a different matter entirely!

77. Stearne, *A Confirmation*, p.13.

78. Hopkins, *A Discovery*, p.5 Earlier in 1645, Stearne was in favour of swimming Elizabeth Clarke in Essex, but it is likely that this was not carried out due to intervention from the magistrates. Serjeant Godbold decreed in 1645 that the swimming of suspected witches was to cease immediately due to the unlawfulness of the practice – swimming a 'witch' was classed as assault, and those involved could be and were prosecuted accordingly. It continued to be carried out on a 'popular' level, with the usual divide between 'learned opinion' on the matter and the beliefs still held by the common people. Well into the nineteenth century, suspected witches found themselves subjected to swimming, with serious repercussions for those who took justice into their own hands.

79. Stearne, p.18.

80. It had suggested that the detailed and self-professed knowledge of witches and their actions held by Hopkins was actually gleaned from the Devil himself, a view that Hopkins was obviously eager to dispel given the implications such an accusation could hold. Hopkins was also rumoured to have brazenly procured the Devil's ledger containing the names of all the witches in England.

81. This point was also corroborated by Stearne, who had clearly read Hopkins' pamphlet and borrowed heavily from the arguments used there, although again one might argue for a somewhat idealised rewriting of events after the fact. One might also muse on whether they had conversations in person, justifying what they were doing during the time of their work or whether this came later – such speculation must, sadly, remain just that.

82. Hopkkins, *A Discovery*, p.9.

83. Hopkins, p.10.

84. Stearne, p.6.

85. Wright, p.24.

86. This fact clearly rankled; Stearne made a plaintive complaint against the fact that he and several others had been 'illegally outlawed' by those who disliked them, without being given a chance to answer to the charges against them. Stearne p.58.

87. Stearne, p.61.
88. EROC, D/P 343/1/1, Gaskill, p.264. As is common with such notorious figures, there have been rumours and sightings across the years that suggest Hopkins remained in his home town after all. The ghost of the witch hunter has been sighted in and around both Mistley and Manningtree, with several spectral forms being identified by witnesses as Hopkins himself.

Chapter 5

1. Gent, Frank J., *The Trial of the Bideford Witches*, Crediton, 2001, p. 25. Ashton, J., *Century of Ballads,* 1887. The full title of this ballad is *Witchcraft Discovered and Punished: Or the trials and condemnation of three notorious witches who were tried at the last Assizes, holden at the Castle of Exeter, in the County of Devon: whereby they received sentence for death, for bewitching several persons, destroying ships at sea, and cattle by land etc.* As to be expected, this source provides a sensationalised but not incredibly accurate account of the case.
2. *A True and Impartial Relation of the Informations Against Three Witches*, London, 1682 p.20.
3. It is unclear from the accounts available the order in which the information was given, and whether Temperance confessed before Thomas Eastchurch officially gave his version of events or vice versa.
4. *A True and Impartial Relation*, p.26.
5. Anne Wakely and Honor Hooper were also in favour of this move and fully supportive of the Eastchurch couple in their belief that Temperance should be questioned further.
6. *Ibid.* p.23.
7. Lydia Burman had given evidence that Temperance had 'appeared unto her in the shape of a red pig at such time as the said Lydia was brewing in the house of one Humphrey Ackland'. *Ibid.* p.23.
8. Gent, Frank J., *The Trial of the Bideford Witches*, p.5.
9. *A True and Impartial Relation*, p.32.
10. It is unclear exactly where this 'confession' overheard by William Edwards took place, and who Susannah was speaking to at the time.
11. *Ibid.* p.34.
12. *Ibid.* p.35.
13. *Ibid.* p.35.
14. *Ibid.* p.35.
15. *Ibid.* p.35.
16. As well as his forms as a man and a boy, the Devil also came to Susannah in the shape of a lion. She also revealed that Mary Trembles was her servant, in the same way that she herself was a servant to the Devil.

NOTES

17. *Ibid.* p.29.
18. *Ibid.* p.36.
19. *Ibid.* p.37. It is interesting that in Joan's account Susannah's identity is only implied by Anthony Jones, whereas in his own account he calls her by name.
20. As already recounted, this had duly been done, but Temperance had been acquitted.
21. *Ibid.* p.27.
22. On the charges against them, Mary and Susannah had both confessed to the same crime, that of tormenting Grace Barnes. The authorities ran into difficulties here, as both women couldn't be indicted on the same offence. Accordingly the matter was solved by indicting Mary Trembles for the suffering of Grace Barnes, whilst Susannah Edwards was indicted for tormenting Dorcas Coleman. Barry, Jonathan, *Witchcraft and Demonism in South West England*, (Palgrave Historical Studies in Witchcraft and Magic) AIAA, 2012, p.65.
23. This interesting addition that is missing from the information given by witnesses against Temperance or her own confessions prior to this could point to accusations and rumours against her that were made after her transfer to Exeter and thus did not appear in earlier evidence or statements.
24. *A True and Impartial Relation*, p.43.
25. *Ibid.* p.43.
26. *Ibid.* p.43.
27. *Ibid.* p.43. The speeches recorded – whether accurate or not – reflect what readers would expect as a fitting end for the women and such justice being served, bringing the whole matter to a satisfying end.
28. The mention of sea and ship related crimes in this account is of interest as it is a common motif from witch trials of the mid-1600s Mary Lakeland, the Ipswich woman accused of witchcraft and husband murder and burned for the latter in 1645 was said to have set ships adrift and caused mayhem amongst mariners. Such accusations as have already been noted in the preceding chapter and featured in the 1645 Bury St Edmund trials. These accusations against the women are absent from the evidence and information gathered in the first pamphlet, but, intriguingly, do feature in the questioning by Mr Hann that comes in the accounts of the executions of the women at the pamphlet's close. Temperance was asked if she or any of her associates had overturned ships or whether she had ridden over an arm of the sea on a cow. It has been suggested that these associations were added to tales of what the witches had done when they were transferred to Exeter and had nothing to do with the original accusations against them. Barry, p.86.
29. Barry, p.80.
30. There is some debate over the date of publication for this account; often read as 1687, it has been argued that this is an error in either printing or reading, and that it was, in fact, printed in 1682 along with the previous two pamphlets.

31. *The Life and Conversation of Temperance Floyd, Mary Lloyd, and Susannah Edwards*, pp.2-5 Temperance was also credited with having admitted to going to sea in an egg shell in order to wreak havoc on the ships there; a popular and enduring piece of folklore where witches and the sea were concerned.

32. Rachel Winslade was the daughter of John Winslade, baptised in Bideford in 1584, making her 28 years old when Susannah was born. John Winslade had at least one other child, an aunt to Susannah.

33. As in so many cases, the families of the accused, especially grown children who played no direct role in the accusations against their parents, Susannah's children are absent from the accounts of the case, leaving an intriguing gap in the story. The Bideford parish registers reveal that Susannah's daughter Unis or Eunice had two illegitimate children, Ruth born January 1665 and Samuel 1671. There is no record of who the father was and no mention of the children or him in the accounts. Susannah also had at least one sister, Jane, born in 1620 although, again, there is no further information on her or the relationship of the two sisters.

34. Barry, Jonathan, *Witchcraft and Demonism in South West England*, (Palgrave Historical Studies in Witchcraft and Magic) AIAA, 2012, p.74.

35. Intriguingly, there were two women baptised with the forename Temperance in Bideford; one Temperance Babacombe, baptised in 1589 (which would put her at over 90 at the time of the trial) and Temperance Gebbons, baptised in 1642, which would make her only 40. It is unlikely that either of these women are therefore candidates for Temperance's identity. There are various others from other areas in Devon who might match the right age, but it is impossible to make more than an educated guess on the matter and Temperance's origins remain unknown.

36. Temperance and Susannah are recorded as receiving aid in 1678, 1679 and 1682, with Mary Trembles receiving relief in 1680, again further evidence that all three women had been in Bideford for some time. Barry, Jonathan, *Witchcraft and Demonism in South West England*, p.74.

37. Gent, p.3.

38. *Ibid*. p.9.

39. *Ibid*. p.4. Interestingly, Grace and Elizabeth Barnes and their father were listed amongst those dissenting in 1674. Barry, *Witchcraft and Demonism in South West England*, p.74.

40. The rector Ogilby was 'abused' by a parishioner during Sunday service on more than one occasion, and was also denounced by his flock on numerous counts, including allowing Mr Hann to preach despite being excommunicated, and for drinking, swearing and being verbally abusive. John Hill was also spoken out against.

41. *A True and Impartial Relation*, p.43. In reply, Temperance related how she had sold apples and had grown angry when a child had taken an apple from her

and the mother, instead of giving it back, had taken it herself from the child. The child had, Temperance insisted, died of smallpox, not of her bewitching. One of the few concrete though hardly conclusive links between the two cases is at a remove, as one of the women who gave evidence against Temperance during her previous accusation for witchcraft, Dorcas Lidstone, now Dorcas Coleman, was one of those to speak out against Susannah and Mary years later. There is no outright evidence to suggest that Temperance was aware of the existence of Susannah and Mary or vice versa.

42. Barry, p.74.

43. What is intriguing is that Elizabeth appears to have been considerably younger than the other women accused at the time, and proof against the stereotype that only old women found themselves in danger of being accused.

44. Interestingly, Mary's mother Grace Beare was a Dallyn by birth, the same surname as one of Temperance Lloyd's supposed victims. It is unclear what, if any, connection there might have been between the families and if this held any relevance to the case.

45. Gent, p.17.

46. It is also an important reminder that not every accusation for witchcraft in England led to execution, especially during the tail end of the witch trial period.

47. Gent, p.12. The idea that the three women were weary of their lives and the suffering that they had to endure, with the additional pressure of the accusations against them, was suggested by Sir Francis North at the time as a reason for the accused from Bideford confessing to the deeds ascribed to them.

48. Gent, p.15.

49. There is nothing to particularly support the speculation that has been made that because her husband, a mariner, was at sea a lot, this was an explanation for her 'distressed' behaviour, although this *does* keenly highlight the way in which women, both past and present, continue to be viewed and judged today.

50. Sir Francis North's communication with Secretary of State Sir Leoline Jenkins is illuminating in this regard; After speculating that the three women appeared weary of their lives and pointing out that the evidence against them was 'very full and fanciful', he went on to say that:

> I find the country so fully possessed against them that although some of the virtuosi may think these the effects of confederacy, melancholy, or delusion, and that young folks are altogether as quick-sighted as they who are old and infirm; yet we cannot reprieve them without appearing to deny the very being of witches, which as it is contrary to law, so I think it would be ill for his Majesty's service, for it may give the faction occasion to afoot the old trade of witchfinding that may cost many innocent persons their lives, which the justice will not prevent.

Ewen, *Witchcraft and Demonism,* pp.372-3.

51. Inderwick, F. A., *Side-Lights on the Stuarts,* London, 1888, p.192. A copy of the relevant extract from the gaol book can be found in Ewen, *Witchcraft and Witch Trials,* p.43.

52. Barry, p.58.

53. There were further accusations of witchcraft in Bideford after this date, and in 1687 informations were taken against Abigail Handford. Nothing more is known of this case, and she does not appear to have been executed. The execution of Temperance, Susannah and Mary was also not the first case of witchcraft to occur in Bideford. In 1658, Grace Ellyot, wife of Josias Ellyot, was bound over for good behaviour after being accused of witchcraft, with apparently no further outcome. Ewen, *Witchcraft and Demonism,* p.441.

54. A 1938 dramatised account was produced by Bruce Seymour, and in recent years, 'Possession: Macbeth' by the Shake-scene players took place in 2005, in 2006 there was a radio play by BBC Radio Devon entitled 'The Witches of Bideford', and the case was mentioned in the notes for a 2008 production of 'Try the Witch' – Barry. p.61. For those who enjoy a ghostly element to their history, the case was also featured on 'Most Haunted'.

55. It is interesting to see how different areas approach their more troubling aspects of history – in contrast, you will be hard pressed to find mention or commemoration of the Belvoir Witches in Lincoln where they were executed in 1619. Also, the mural itself has caused controversy as there are many who believe the depiction of the witches with their stereotyped witches garb and cauldron is insensitive, sexist and outdated.

56. The archived petition can be found at https://petition.parliament.uk/archived/petitions/37616.